Vest Pocket
ITALIAN

Formerly published as: ITALIAN IN A NUTSHELL

By
DR. NICHOLAS J. MILELLA
Department of Romance Languages.
City College of New York

PUBLISHED BY

INSTITUTE FOR LANGUAGE STUDY
Westport, Connecticut 06880

DISTRIBUTED TO THE BOOK TRADE BY
HENRY HOLT & COMPANY

Library of Congress Cataloging-in-Publication Data

Milella, Nicholas J.
  Vest Pocket Italian.

  Previously published as: Italian in a Nutshell.
   1. Italian language—Conversation and phrase books
—English. 2. Italian language—Grammar—1950–
3. Italian language—Dictionaries—English. 4. English
language—Dictionaries—Italian. I. Title.
PC1121.M48 1989   458.3'421   89–15366
ISBN 0-8489-5104-2

Printed in the United States of America

HH Editions 9 8 7 6 5 4 3 2   *9104-10

GETTING THE MOST OUT OF YOUR COURSE

THE WORLD is growing smaller every day. Far-sighted people who recognize the value of speaking a second language will reap the benefits of greater business success, more traveling enjoyment, easier study and finer social relationships.

VEST POCKET ITALIAN will unlock for you the treasure house of learning a language the easy way, with a fresh, new approach—without monotonous drills. Before you know it, you'll be speaking your new language easily and without embarrassment. You will be able to converse with fascinating people from other lands and read books and magazines from their country in the original language.

Much research and painstaking study has gone into the "Vest Pocket" method of learning a new language as easily as possible. This Course is the result of that research, and for the reader's convenience it is divided into several basic, closely related sections:

The KEY TO PRONUNCIATION explains the sounds of the language. Each sentence is accompanied by the phonetic spelling to help you learn the pronunciation. This method has been tested extensively and is found to be the best to enable the student to associate sounds with written forms.

The BASIC SENTENCE PATTERNS are the unique new approach to sentence construction. Here you will find sentence patterns needed in general conversation. On these basic patterns you can build sentences to suit your own particular needs.

The EVERYDAY CONVERSATIONS form the main section of this book. Here you will find a large number of situations useful for general language learning and traveling purposes. You will learn hundreds upon hundreds of conversational sentences you may need to make yourself understood. Even more important, the material is organized to provide you with a wide basis for varying the vocabulary and sentences as much as your interest and ingenuity might desire.

The OUTLINE OF GRAMMAR provides a rapid understanding of the grammatical structure of your new language. The "Basic Sentence Patterns" are closely correlated with this section to give you a quick knowledge of the language.

The two-way DICTIONARY of over 6500 entries includes all the words used in the Everyday Conversations and contains another 3000 frequently used words and expressions. It thus forms a compact and invaluable tool for the student.

Here are the tools. Use them systematically, and before you know it you will have a "feeling" for the new language. The transcriptions furnish authentic reproduction of the language to train your ear and tongue to the foreign sounds; thus you can SEE the phrase, SAY the phrase, HEAR the phrase, and LEARN the phrase.

Remember that repetition and practice are the foundation stones of language learning. Repeat and practice what you have learned as often as you can. You will be amazed (and your friends will, too) how quickly you have acquired a really practical knowledge of Italian.

THE EDITORS

TABLE OF CONTENTS

Outline of Italian Grammar

Italian—English Dictionary

KEY TO ITALIAN PRONUNCIATION

The sounds of Italian are easy to master for Americans, because all these vowels and consonants occur in English also. A careful reading of the following instructions will help you greatly in acquiring a correct pronunciation.

VOWELS

There are seven vowel sounds in Italian:

ITALIAN SPELLING	PHONETIC SYMBOL	DESCRIPTION	EXAMPLE
a	ah	As in *father* or *barter*.	*lacrima* (lah'-kri-mah), tear
e	e	As in *they* or *a* in *fate*, but without any diphthongal glide.	*fedele* (fe-de'-le), faithful
e	è	As in *met* or *bred*. (Can occur in stressed syllables *only*.)	*medico* (mè-di-ko), physician
i	i	As in *machine* or *ee* in *peel*. (Note this carefully to avoid giving it any other value. The only change occurs in the unstressed combinations *ia, ie, io* and *iu,* transcribed as *ya, ye, yo* and *yu* to represent the combined sound. Similarly, *ai, ei,* etc., are transcribed *ah-y, è-y,* etc.)	*piccolo* (pik'-ko-lo), small

7

ITALIAN SPELLING	PHONETIC SYMBOL	DESCRIPTION	EXAMPLE
o	o	As in *grow* or *dome*, but without any diphthongal glide.	*solo* (so'-lo), alone
o	ò	As in *north*. (Can occur in stressed syllables *only*.)	*poco* (pò-ko), little, few *forte* (fòr-te), strong
u	u	As in *rule* or *oo* in *loop*. (Note this carefully to avoid giving it different values as is done in English. The only change occurs in the unstressed combinations *ua, ue, ui* and *uo*, transcribed as *wa, we, wi* and *wo* to represent the combined sound.)	*zucchero* (tsuk'-ke-ro), sugar *uva* (u'-vah), grape

CONSONANTS

The consonants *b, d, f, l, m, n, p, q, t* and *v* are pronounced approximately as in English. However, always take care to articulate them clearly, and keep in mind that the *p* and the *t*, as well as the sound of *k*, should not be aspirated as in English.

ITALIAN SPELLING	PHONETIC SYMBOL	DESCRIPTION	EXAMPLE
c	k	As in *cat* or *cot* before *a, o* or *u* as well as before consonants, including *h*.	*Carlo* (kahr'-lo), Charles *credere* (kre'-de-re), to believe *che* (ke), what, that *chi* (ki), who
c	ch	As in *cheese* or *chin* before *e* or *i*.	*cena* (che'-nah), supper *cinque* (chin'-kwe), five

ITALIAN SPELLING	PHONETIC SYMBOL	DESCRIPTION	EXAMPLE
g	g	As in *girl* or *go* before *a, o* or *u* as well as before consonants, including *h*.	*gatto* (gaht'-to), cat *ghiaccio* (gyah'-cho), ice *gridare* (gri-dah'-re), to shout
g	j	As in *gem* or *manage* before *e* or *i*.	*gettare* (jet-tah'-re), to throw *giallo* (jahl'-lo), yellow
gl	ly	As *lli* in *million*, except in a few words as *negligente* and *glicerina*.	*maraviglioso* (mah-rah-vi-lyo'-zo), marvellous *egli* (e'-lyi), he
gn	ny	As *ny* in *canyon*.	*bagno* (bah'-nyo), bath
h	—	Always silent; its only function is to modify the pronunciation of the *c* and the *g* (see above).	*ho* (ò), I have *ha* (ah), (he) has
r	r	Always trilled, somewhat as in British pronunciation of *very;* pronounce in front of mouth, quickly vibrating tongue against upper teeth.	*ripresa* (ri-pre'-zah), renewal, repetition
s	s	As in *sole* (voiceless)	*suono* (swò-no), sound
s	z	As in *zeal* (voiced)	*bisogno* (bi-zo'-nyo), need *sbaglio* (zbah'-lyo), error
sc	sh	As in *shell* before *e* or *i*.	*scelta* (shel'-tah), choice
sc	sk	As in *skull* before *a, o* or *u* as well as before consonants, including *h*.	*scarpa* (skahr'-pah), shoe *scherzo* (skèr-tso), joke *schiuma* (skyu'-mah), foam
z	ts	As in *pots*.	*grazie* (grah'-tsye), thank you
z	dz	As in *suds*.	*zelo* (dzè-lo), zeal

DOUBLE CONSONANTS

In Italian the double consonants are pronounced more vigorously than the single ones, and are of longer duration. In our phonetic transcription the first of the double consonants is written at the end of the preceding syllable, but make sure to produce one single sound in your pronunciation.

The following pairs of words wil. illustrate the difference in sound between single and double consonants:

eco (è-ko), echo : *ecco* (èk-ko), here is, there is

belo (bè-lo), bleating : *bello* (bèl-lo), beautiful

cometa (ko-mè-tah), comet : *commetta* (kom-met'-tah) , he may commit

sono (so'-no), they are : *sonno* (son'-no), sleep

napo (nah'-po), turnip : *nappo* (nahp'-po), cup

caro (kah'-ro), dear : *carro* (kahr'-ro), car

fato (fah'-to), fate , *fatto* (faht'-to), made

ACCENT

The accent in the phonetic transcription is indicated with an (') following the stressed syllable. This accent is not indicated in stressed syllables containing an open *e* or *o* (*è, ò*), because these two sounds can occur *only* in stressed syllables.

The rules concerning the position of the stressed syllable in Italian words are as follows: The accent usually falls on the next to the last syllable. However, some words are accented on the third, or even fourth or fifth, from the last syllable, whereas other words are accented on the final syllable, in which case they usually take a grave accent (*à, è, ì, ò, ù*) on the vowel of that last syllable. The grave accent is also used to distinguish between words of identical spelling but different meaning: *àncora* (anchor), *ancora* (still, yet).

BASIC SENTENCE PATTERNS

In each language there are a few basic types of sentences which are used more often than others in everyday speech.

On the basis of such sentences, it is possible to form many others by substituting one or two of each of these basic sentences. The phrases and sentences selected to illustrate the basic patterns are short, easy to memorize and useful. Learning them before you tackle the main section of the book with the phrases covering everyday needs and travel situations, you will acquire an idea of the structure of the language. You will also learn indirectly through these basic types of sentences some of the most important grammatical categories and their function in the construction of the sentences the natural way—the way they are encountered in actual usage.

Cross references have been supplied to establish a correlation between the basic sentence patterns and the Grammar section in this book. This will help you to relate the grammatical knowledge you'll acquire passively going through the sentences to the systematic presentation of the basic facts of grammar. For example, when you encounter the phrase "See 4.4" in the first group of sentences, it means that by turning to Chapter 4, subdivision 4 in the Grammar section you will find a description of the interrogative pronouns and their uses.

BASIC QUESTIONS AND ANSWERS
(See 4.4; 4.1; 4.3; 2.1, 2.3)

Who is he?	He is my father (uncle, grandfather).
Chi è?	**È mio padre (zio, nonno).**
ki è?	*è mi'-o pah'-dre (tsi'-o, nòn-no).*
Who is she?	She is my mother (aunt, grandmother).
Chi è (lei)?	**È mia madre (zia, nonna).**
ki è (lè-y)?	*è mi'-a mah'-dre (tsi'-a, nòn-na).*

Who is that boy?
Chi è quel ragazzo?
ki è kwel rah-gah'-tso?

He is my brother (cousin, nephew).
È mio fratello (cugino, nipote).
è mi'-o frah-tèl-lo (ku-ji'-no, ni-pò-te).

Who is the other boy?
Chi è l'altro ragazzo? (See 3.1-3)
ki è lahl'-tro rah-gah'-tso?

That's my older brother.
È mio fratello maggiore. (See 3.4)
è mi'-o frah-tèl-lo mah-jo'-re.

Who is that girl?
Chi è quella ragazza?
ki è kwel'-lah rah-gah'-tsah?

She is my younger sister (cousin, niece).
È mia sorella minore (cugina, nipote).
è mi'-ah so-rèl-lah mi-no'-re (ku-ji'-nah, ni-pò-te).

Who are they?
Chi sono?
ki so'-no?

They are my grandparents.
Sono i miei nonni.
so'-no i myè-y nòn-ni.

That tall girl is my girl friend.
Quella ragazza alta è la mia amica. (See 4.5)
kwel'-lah rah-gah'-tsah ahl'-tah è lah mi'-ah ah-mi'-kah

Is that so?
Non mi dica?
non mi di'-kah?

Where is my hat?
Dov'è il mio cappello? (See 6.3)
do-vè il mi'-o kahp-pèl-lo?

Here it is.
Eccolo qua.
èk-ko-lo kwah.

Where is your briefcase?
Dov'è la sua valigetta?
do-vè lah su'-ah vah-li-jet'-tah?

It's over here.
E' qui.
è kwi.

Where's her suitcase?
Dov'è la sua valigia?
do-vè lah su'-ah vah-li'-jah?

It's over there.
E' la.
è lah.

Where's the washroom?
Dov'è il gabinetto (la ritirata)?
do-vè il gah-bi-net'-to (lah ri-ti-rah'-tah)?

It's on the right (on the left).
E' a destra (a sinistra).
è ah de'-strah (ah si-ni'-strah).

Where is John's room?
Dov'è la camera di Giovanni?
do-vè lah kah'-me-rah di jo-vahn'-ni?

It's straight ahead.
E' avanti diritto.
è ah-vahn'-ti di-rit'-to.

Where is Mary's room?
Dov'è la camera di Maria?
do-vè lah kah'-me-rah di mah-ri'-ah?

It's one flight up.
E' al primo piano.
è ahl pri'-mo pyah'-no.

(See also 4.5)

Who has my notebooks? Paul has them.
Chi ha i miei quaderni? Paolo li ha.
ki ah i myè-y kwah-dèr-ni? pah'-o-lo li ah.

With whom were you talking? With my friend Peter.
Con chi parlava Lei? Col mio amico Pietro.
kon ki pahr-lah'-vah lè-y? kol mi'-o ah-mi'-ko pyè-tro.

Who are those men? They are my son's friends.
Chi sono quei signori? Sono gli amici di mio figlio.
ki so'-no kwè-y si-nyo'-ri? so'-no lyi ah-mi'-chi di mi'-o fi-lyo.

Who are those girls? They are my daughter's schoolmates.
Chi sono quelle ragazze? Sono le compagne di scuola di mia figlia.
*ki so'-no kwel'-le rah-gah'-tse? so'no le kom-pah'-nye di skwò-lah di
        mi'-ah fi'-lyah.*

What did she say? She said she couldn't come.
Che cosa ha detto? Ha detto che non è potuto venire.
ke kò-zah ah dèt-to? ah dèt-to ke non è po-tu'-to ve-ni'-re.

What is your occupation? I am a salesman.
Qual' è la sua occupazione? Sono commesso.
kwahl è lah su'-ah ok-ku-pah-tsi-o'-ne? so'-no kom-mes'-so.

Which one of these books do you like best? This one.
Quale di questi libri preferisce (le piace di più)? Questo.
kwah'-le di kwe'-sti li'-bri pre-fe-ri'-she (le pyah'-che di pyu)? kwe'-sto.

What is love? It's a wonderful thing.
Che cosa è l'amore? E'una cosa meravigliosa.
ke kò-sah è lah-mo'-re? è u'-nah kò'-sah me-ra-vi-lyo'-sah.

SENTENCES WITH *HIM, HER* AND *IT*
(PERSONAL OBJECT PRONOUNS)
(See 4.1; 9.1; 9.3, 9.4)

John gave it to him.
Giovanni glielo ha dato (gliel'ha dato).
jo-vahn'-ni lye'-lo ah dah'-to (lye'-lah dah'-to).

He gave it to me.
Me lo ha dato. (Me l'ha dato).
me lo ah dah'-to. (me lah dah'-to).

I gave it to her.
Gliel'ho dato.
lye'-lò dah'-to.

She sent it to us.
Ce lo ha mandato. (Ce l'ha mandato).
che lo ah mahn-dah'-to. (che lah mahn-dah'-to).

We gave it to you.
Glielo abbiamo dato. (Gliel'abbiamo dato).
lye'-lo ahb-byah'-mo dah'-to. (lye-lahb-byah'-mo dah'-to).

You did not give it to them.
Non lo ha dato loro.
non lo ah dah'-to lo'-ro.

Give it to me.
Me lo dia.
me lo di'-ah.

Don't give it to him.
Non glielo dia.
non lye'-lo di'-ah.

Send it to her.
Glielo mandi.
lye'-lo mahn'-di.

Mail it to us.
Ce lo mandi (spedisca).
che lo mahn'-di (spe-di'-skah).

Don't mail it to them.
Non lo spedisca loro.
non lo spe-di'-skah lo-ro.

SENTENCES ON THE USE OF *THE*, *AN* AND *A*

(*The Articles*, See 1.1-6)

The books, the pencil, the pen and the erasers are on the desk.
I libri, il lapis, la penna e le gomme stanno sulla scrivania.
I li'-bri, il lah'-pis, lah pen'nah e le gom'-me stahn'-no sul-lah skri-vah - ni'-ah.

The clock and the mirror are antiques.
L'orologio e lo specchio sono antichi.
lo-ro-lò-jo e lo spèk-kyo so'-no ahn-ti'-ki.

The students live at 900 Fourth Avenue.
Gli studenti abitano al numero novecento del Viale Quattro.
lyi stu-dèn-ti ah-bi'-tah-no ahl nu'-me-ro no- e-chèn-to del viah'-le kwaht'-tro.

I bought a sofa, a table and some chairs of the same style.
Ho comprato un divano, una tavola e delle sedie dello stesso stile.
ò kom-prah'-to un di-vah'-no, u'-nah tah'-vo-lah e del'-le sè-dye del'-lo stes'-so sti'-le.

Italy is one of the most beautiful countries in Europe.
L'Italia è uno dei più bei paesi d'Europa.
li-tah'-lyah è u'-no de'-y pyu be'-i pah-è-zi de-u-rò-pah.

It costs 200 lire a pound.
Costa duecento lire la libbra.
kò-stah du-e-chèn-to li'-re lah lib'-brah.

He is a musician.
Fa il musicista.
fah il mu-zi-chi'-sta.

What a fool!
Che sciocco! (See 8.2)
ke shòk-ko!

What a pity!
Che peccato!
ke pek-kah'-to!

SENTENCES USING *ANYBODY* AND *ANYTHING*
(*The Indefinite Pronouns*, See 4.6)

Has anybody come? Nobody has come.
E' venuto qualcuno? Nessuno è venuto.
è ve-nu'-to kwahl-ku'-no? nes-su'-no è ve-nu'-to.

Has anybody been here? Somebody has been here.
C'è stato qualcuno qui? Qualcuno è stato qui.
chè stah'-to kwahl-ku'-no kwi? kwahl-ku'-no è stah'-to kwi.

Have you received any letters? Yes, I received some.
Ha ricevuto delle lettere? Sì, ne ho ricevute alcune.
ah ri-che-vu'-to del'-le lèt-te-re? si, ne ò ri-che-vu'-te ahl-ku'-ne.

No, I have not received any.
No, non ne ho ricevute.
no, non ne ò ri-che-vu'-te.

Have you got any American magazines? Yes, I have some.
Ha delle riviste americane? Sì, ne ho alcune.
ah del'-le ri-vi'-ste ah-me-ri-kah'-ne? si, ne ò ahl-ku'-ne.

There is one.
Eccone una.
èk-ko-ne u'nah.

Have you any English newspapers? I'm sorry. I don't have any.
Ha dei giornali inglesi? Mi dispiace. Non ne ho.
ah de'-y jor-nah'-li in-gle'-zi? mi dis-pyah'-che. non ne ò.

Have you got a match? Sorry. No.
Vuol favorirmi un fiammifero? Mi dispiace. Non ne ho.
vwòl fah-vo-rir'-mi un fyahm-mi'-fe-ro? mi dis-pyah'-che. non ne ò.

Do you sell milk here? Yes. We do. Please give me a bottle.
Si vende del latte qui? Sì, ne vendiamo. Per piacere me ne dia un litro.
si ven'-de del laht'-te kwi? si, ne ven-dyah'-mo.
    per pyah-che'-re me ne di'-ah un li-tro.

Have you got any money? No, I have no money.
Ha del denaro? No, non ho denaro.
ah del de-nah'-ro? no, non ò de-nah'-ro.

What did you eat? I ate some cheese.
Che cosa ha mangiato? Ho mangiato del formaggio (cacio).
ke kò-zah ah mahn-jah'-to? ò mahn-jah'-to del for-mah'-joh (kah'-cho).

What did you buy? I bought some dresses and a suit.
Che cosa ha comprato? Ho comprato delle vesti ed un abito.
ke kò-zah ah kom-prah'-to? ò kom-prah'-to del'-le ve'-sti ed un ah'-bi-to.

SENTENCES ON ADJECTIVES
(See 3.1-4, especially 3.4)

Helen is taller than Mary.
Elena è più alta di Maria.
e-le'-nah è pyu ahl'-tah di mah-ri'-ah.

Alice is less humorous than Betty.
Alice è meno spiritosa di Bettina.
ah-li'-che è me'-no spi-ri-tò-zah di bet-ti'-nah.

Catherine is as tall as Mary.
Caterina è (tanto) alta quanto Maria.
kah-te-ri'-nah è (tahn'-to) ahl'-tah kwahn'-to mah-ri'-ah.

Kate is not so tall as Mary.
Rina non è (tanto) alta quanto Maria.
ri'-nah non è (tahn'-to) ahl'-tah kwahn'-to ma-ri'-ah.

Ann is the tallest of the girls.
Anna è la più alta delle ragazze.
ahn'-nah è lah pyu ahl'-tah del'-le rah-gah'-tse.

This street has more traffic.
Questa strada ha più traffico.
kwe'-stah strah'-dah ah pyu trahf'-fi-ko.

I will take a little more meat.
Prenderò un po' più di carne.
pren-de-rò un pò pyu di kahr'-ne.

Please have some more.
Ne prenda ancora.
ne prèn-dah ahn-ko'-rah.

I don't want any more.
Non ne desidero più.
non ne de-zi-de-ro pyu.

They don't want to stay here any longer.
Non vogliono rimanere più qui.
non vò-lyo-no ri-mah-ne'-re pyu kwi.

He can no longer go there.
Non può più andare là.
non pwò pyu ahn-dah'-re lah.

My tall friend owns a new red car.
Il mio amico alto possiede una nuova automobile rossa.
il mi'-o ah-mi'-ko ahl'-to pos-sye'-de u'-nah nwo'-vah au-to-mò-bi-le ros'-sah.

The old Italian doctor didn't come to see us.
Il vecchio medico italiano non è venuto a visitarci.
il vèk-kyo mè-di-ko i-tah-li-ah'-no non è ve-nu'-to ah vi-zi-tahr'-chi.

BASIC TYPES OF SENTENCES

(See 9.1)

Affirmative: This lesson is easy.
Questa lezione è facile.
kwe'-stah le-tsyo'-ne è fah'-chi-le.

Negative: This lesson is not difficult.
Questa lezione non è difficile.
kwe'-stah le-tsyo'-ne non è dif-fi'-chi-le.

Interrogative: Is this lesson easy?
E' facile questa lezione?
è fah'-chi-le kwe'-stah le-tsyo'-ne?

It's easy.
E' facile.
è fah'-chi-le.

Isn't this room large?
Non è grande questa stanza?
non è grahn'-de kwe'-stah stahn'-tsah?

Yes, it's large.
Sì, è grande.
si, è grahn'-de.

I gave Mary the book.
Ho dato il libro a Maria.
ò dah'-to il li'-bro ah mah-ri'-ah.

I gave it to Mary.
L'ho dato a Maria.
lò dah'-to ah mah-ri'-ah.

I gave it to him.
L'ho dato a lui.
lò dah'-to ah lu'-y.

She went there.
E' andata là.
è ahn-dah'-tah lah.

Did he go there?
E' andato là?
è ahn-dah'-to lah?

He didn't go there.
Non è andato là.
non è ahn-dah'-to lah.

Didn't they go there?
Non sono andati là?
non so'-no ahn-dah'-ti lah?

Yes, they did.
Sì, ci sono andati.
si, chi so'-no ahn-dah'-ti.

Who wants to go to school?
Chi vuole andare a scuola?
ki vu-ò-le ahn-dah'-re ah skwò-lah?

I want to go to school.
Io voglio andare a scuola.
i'-o vò-lyo ahn-dah'-re ah skwò-lah.

You don't want to go to school.
(Lei) Non vuole andare a scuola.
(lè-y) non vu-ò-le ahn-dah'-re ah skwò-lah.

Do they really want to go to school?
Vogliono proprio andare a scuola?
vò-lyo-no pro'-pri-o ahn-dah'-re ah skwò-lah?

WHO, WHOM AND CONDITIONAL CLAUSES
(Relative Pronouns; See 4.7; 9.2)

Those who study languages with records can pronounce them correctly
   and learn them more easily.
**Chi studia le lingue coi dischi può pronunziarle correttamente e
   apprenderle più facilmente.**
*ki stu-di'-ah le lin'-gu-e ko'-y di'-ski pu-ò pro-nun-tzi-ahr'-le
   kor-ret-tah-mèn-te e ahp-prèn-der-le pyu fah-chil-men'-te.*

Who is the lady with whom I saw you last night?
Chi è la signora con la quale la vidi ieri sera?
ki è lah si-nyo'-rah kon lah kwah'-le lah vi'-di iè-ri se'-rah?

She is my aunt who just came from Europe.
E' mia zia che è appena arrivata dall' Europa.
è mi'-ah tsi'-ah ke è ahp-pe'-nah ahr-ri-vah'-tah dahl-leu-rò-pah.

The girl to whom I was speaking is my fiancee.
La ragazza con cui parlavo è la mia fidanzata.
lah rah-gah'-tsah kon ku'-i pahr-lah-vo è lah mi'-ah fi-dahn-tsah'-tah.

The boy whose father is my teacher lives here.
Il ragazzo il cui padre è mio maestro abita qui.
il rah-gah'-tso il ku-i pah'-dre è mì'-o mah-è-stro ah-bi'-tah kwi.

Don't tell me that this blue book is not yours.
Non mi dica che questo libro blu non è suo.
non mi di'-kah ke kwe'-sto li'-bro blu non è su'-o.

When she came, he left.
Quando venne lei, se ne andò lui.
kwahn'-do ven'-ne lè-y, se ne ahn-dò lu'-y.

If John comes, I will tell it to him.
Se viene Giovanni, glielo dirò.
se vyè-ne jo-vahn'-ni, lye'-lo di-rò.

If John came, I would tell it to him.
Se Giovanni venisse, glielo direi.
se jo-vahn'-ni ve-nis'-se, lye'-lo di-rè-y.

If John had come, I would have told it to him.
Se Giovanni fosse venuto, glielo avrei detto.
se jo-vahn'-ni fos'-se ve-nu'-to, lye'-lo ah-vrè-y dèt-to.

When John comes, I will talk to him about it.
Quando verrà Giovanni, gliene parlerò.
kwahn'-do ver-rah' jo-vahn'-ni, lye'-ne pahr-le-rò.

When John came, I told him the news.
Quando Giovanni è venuto, gli ho dato la notizia.
kwahn'-do jo-vahn'-ni è ve-nu'-to, lyi ò dah'-to lah no-ti'-tsi-ah.

It is probable (that) the train will arrive on time.
E' probabile che il treno arrivi in orario. (See 9.2)
è pro-bah'-bi-le ke il trè-no ahr-ri'-vi in o-rah'-ri-o.

It was probable (that) the train would arrive on time.
Era probabile che il treno arrivasse in orario.
è-rah pro-bah'-bi-le ke il trè-no ahr-ri-vahs'-se in o-rah'-ri-o.

I don't find anyone who is willing to go.
Non trovo nessuno che sia disposto ad andare.
non trò-vo nes-su'-no ke si'-ah dis-pòs-to ahd ahn-dah'-re.

I didn't find anyone who was willing to go.
Non ho trovato nessuno che fosse disposto ad andare.
non ò tro-vah'-to nes-su'-no ke fos'-se dis-pòs-to ahd ahn-dah'-re.

EVERYDAY CONVERSATIONS

BASIC EXPRESSIONS

Good morning. Good evening. Good night.
Buon giorno. **Buona sera.** **Buona sera (Buona notte).**
bwòn jor'-no. *bwò-nah se'-rah.* *bwò-nah se'-rah (bwò-nah not'-te).*

Goodbye. Hello.
Arrivederci (Arrivederla). **Buon giorno (ciao).**
ahr-ri-ve-der'-chi (ahr-ri-ve-der'-lah). *bwòn jor'-no (chah'-o).*

Thank you. You're welcome. Excuse me.
Grazie. **Prego (non c'è di che; s'immagini).** **Mi scusi.**
grah'-tsye. *pre'-go (non chè di ke; sim-mah'-ji-ni).* *mi sku'-zi.*

Please. How much? Where? When?
Per piacere (per favore). **Quanto?** **Dove?** **Quando?**
per pya-che'-re (per fah-vo'-re). *kwahn'-to?* *do'-ve?* *kwahn'-do?*

I want. Give me. Where is Gina? Where are they?
Desidero. **Mi dia.** **Dov'è Gina?** **Dove sono essi?**
de-zi'-de-ro. *mi di'-ah.* *do-vè ji'-nah?* *do'-ve so'-no es'-si?*

My name is George. Do you speak English? I don't understand.
Mi chiamo Giorgio. **Parla inglese?** **Non capisco.**
mi kyah'-mo jor'-jo. *pahr'-lah in-gle'-ze?* *non kah-pi'-sko.*

Speak more slowly. How do you do?
Parli più adagio (piano). **Come sta?**
pahr'-li pyu ah-dah'-jo (pyah'-no). *ko'-me stah?*

GETTING ACQUAINTED

May I present Mr. (Mrs., Miss) Lanza.
Permetta che le presenti il Signor (la Signora, la Signorina) Lanza.
per-met'-tah ke le pre-zen'-ti il si-nyor (la si-nyo'-rah, lah si-nyo-ri'nah) lahn'-tsah.

(This is) my wife.	And this is my son (daughter).
(Quest'è) mia moglie.	**(E quest'è) mio figlio (mia figlia).**
(kwe-stè) mi'-ah mo'-lye.	*(e kwe-stè) mi'-o fi'-lyo (mi'-ah fi'-lya).*

You speak Italian, I see.	A little, but quite poorly, I'm afraid.
Vedo che parla italiano.	**Un poco, ma temo malissimo.**
ve'-do ke pahr'-lah i-tah-li-ah'-no.	*un pò-ko, mah tè-mo mah-lis'-si-mo.*

Not at all. Can you understand what I'm saying?
Tutt'altro. Capisce ciò che dico?
tut-tahl'-tro. kah-pi'-she cho ke di'-ko?

Is this your first trip to Italy?
È questo il suo primo viaggio in Italia?
è kwe'-sto il su'-o pri'-mo vyaj'-jo in i-tah'-li-ah?

Yes, my first trip.	Are you enjoying yourself?
Sì, è il mio primo viaggio.	**Si sta divertendo?**
si, è il mi'-o pri'-mo vyahj'-jo.	*si stah di-ver-tèn-do?*

Very much. I like the country.
Sì, moltissimo. Mi piace questo paese.
si, mol-tis'-si-mo. mi pyah'-che kwe'-sto pah-e'-ze.

Where do you live in the United States?
Dove abita negli Stati Uniti?
do've ah'-bi-tah ne'-lyi stah'-ti u-ni'-ti?

If you ever come my way, call·upon me.
Se mai passasse dalle mie parti, mi chiami.
se mah'-y pahs-sahs'-se dahl'-le mi'-e pahr'-ti, mi kyah'-mi.

Very kind of you. I hope I shall be able to accept.
Lei è molto gentile. Mi auguro di poter accettare.
lè-y è mol'-to jen-ti'-le. mi ah'-u-gu-ro di po-ter' ah-chet-tah'-re.

Perhaps we can have lunch.
Potremmo far colazione insieme.
po-trem'-mo fahr ko-lah-tsyo'-ne in-syè-me.

Or an apéritif before you leave.
O prendere un aperitivo prima che lei parta.
o prèn-de-re un ah-pe-ri-ti'-vo·pri'-mah ke lè-y pahr'-tah.

COUNTING

one **uno** *un'-o*	six **sei** *sè-y*	eleven **undici** *un'-di-chi*	sixteen **sedici** *se'-di-chi*
two **due** *du'-e*	seven **sette** *sèt-te*	twelve **dodici** *do'-di-chi*	seventeen **diciassette** *di-chas-sèt-te*
three **tre** *tre*	eight **otto** *òt-to*	thirteen **tredici** *tre'-di-chi*	eighteen **diciotto** *di-chòt-to*
four **quattro** *kwaht'-tro*	nine **nove** *nò-ve*	fourteen **quattordici** *kwaht-tor'-di-chi*	nineteen **diciannove** *di-chahn-nò-ve*
five **cinque** *chin'-kwe*	ten **dieci** *dyè-chi*	fifteen **quindici** *kwin'-di-chi*	twenty **venti** *ven'-ti*

---

twenty-one **ventuno** *ven-tu'-no*	forty **quaranta** *kwah-rahn'-tah*	seventy-one **settantuno** *set-tahn-tu'-no*	ninety-one **novantuno** *no-vahn-tu'-no*
twenty-two **ventidue** *ven-ti-du'-e*	fifty **cinquanta** *chin-kwahn-tah*	eighty **ottanta** *ot-tahn'-tah*	one hundred **cento** *chèn-to*
thirty **trenta** *tren'-tah*	sixty **sessanta** *ses-sahn'-tah*	eighty-one **ottantuno** *ot-tahn-tu'-no*	one thousand **mille** *mil'-le*
thirty-one **trentuno** *tren-tu'-no*	seventy **settanta** *set-tahn'-tah*	ninety **novanta** *no-vahn'-tah*	one million **un milione** *un mi-lyo'-ne*

The Ordinal Numerals

first **primo** *pri'-mo*	second **secondo** *se-kon'-do*	third **terzo** *tèr'-tso*	fourth **quarto** *kwahr'-to*	fifth **quinto** *kwin'-to*	sixth **sesto** *sès-to*	seventh **settimo** *sèt-ti-mo*
eighth **ottavo** *ot-tah'-vo*	ninth **nono** *nò-no*	tenth **decimo** *dè-chi-mo*	eleventh **undicesimo** *un-di-chè-zi-mo*		twelfth **dodicesimo** *do-di-chè-zi-mo*	

The Fractions

half, a half	a third	one fourth
mezzo, metà	**un terzo**	**un quarto**
mè-dzo, me-tah'	*un tèr-tso*	*un kwahr'-to*
three quarters	one eighth	one fifteenth
tre quarti	**un ottavo**	**un quindicesimo**
tre kwahr'-ti	*un ot-tah'-vo*	*un kwin-di-chè-zi-mo*

STRANGER IN TOWN

Emergencies

Is there anyone here who speaks English?
C'è qualcuno qui che parli inglese?
chè kwahl-ku'-no kwi ke pahr'-li in-gle'-ze?

I've lost my way.
Mi sono smarrito (Ho perduto la strada).
mi so'-no zmahr-ri'-to (ò per-du'-to lah strah'-dah).

Where do you want to go?
Dove vuole andare?
do'-ve vwò-le ahn-dah'-rè?

Do you understand me?
Mi capisce?
mi kah-pi'-she?

No, I don't understand.
No, non capisco.
no, non kah-pi'-sko.

Please speak slowly.
Per favore, parli adagio.
per fah-vo'-re pahr'-li ah-dah'-jo.

Please repeat.
Mi faccia il favore di ripetere.
mi fah'-chah il fah-vo'-re di ri-pe'-te-re.

What are you saying?
Che cosa dice?
ke kò-sa di'-che?

I can't find my wallet.
Non trovo il portafogli.
non tro'-vo il por-tah-fo'-lyi.

I've been robbed!
Sono stato derubato.
so-no stah'-to de-ru-bah'-to.

Call the police!
Chiami una guardia.
kyah'-mi u'-nah gwahr'-dyah.

Where is the Police Station?	That way.	Police!	Help!	Fire!
Dov'è la Questura?	**È di là.**	**Guardia!**	**Aiuto!**	**Fuoco!**
do'vè lah kwes-tu'-rah?	*è di-lah'!*	*gwahr'-dyah!*	*ah-yu'-to!*	*fwò-ko!*

Take me to the American consul.
Mi conduca dal console americano.
mi kon-du'-kah dahl kon'-so-le ah-me-ri-kah'no.

I've left my overcoat on the train.
Ho lasciato il soprabito in treno.
ò lah-shah'-to il so-prah'-bi-to in trè-no.

How can I get it back?
Come posso riaverlo?
ko'-me pòs-so ryah-ver'-lo?

Can you tell me where the lost and found desk is?
Può dirmi dov'è l'ufficio oggetti rinvenuti?
pwò dir'-mi do-vè' luf-fi'-cho oj-jèt-ti rin-ve-nu'-ti?

I cannot find my hotel.
Non riesco a trovare il mio albergo.
non ryès-ko ah tro-vah'-re il mi'-o ahl-ber'-go.

Can you help me?
Può aiutarmi?
pwò ah-yu-tahr'-mi?

Don't bother me or I will call a policeman.
Non mi secchi, o chiamo una guardia.
non mi sek'-ki, o kyah'-mo u'-nah gwahr'-dyah.

Where are you taking me?
Dove mi sta conducendo?
do'-ve mi stah kon-du-chèn-do?

To the police station. You are under arrest.
Alla questura; Lei è in istato d'arresto.
ahl'-lah kwes-tu'-rah. lè-y è in is-tah'-to dahr-rest'-to.

I need a lawyer.
Ho bisogno d'un avvocato.
ò bi-zo'-nyo dun ahv-vo-kah'-to.

I would like to use the phone.
Vorrei fare una telefonata.
vor-re'-y fah'-re u'-nah te-le-fo-nah'-tah.

I've lost my umbrella.
Ho perduto l'ombrello.
ò per-du'-to lom-brel'lo.

Are you hurt?
Si è fatto male?
si è faht'-to mah'-le?

We should send for a policeman.
Dovremmo far chiamare una guardia.
do-vrem'-mo fahr kyah-mah'-re u'-nah gwahr'-dyah.

Please let me have your name and address.
Per favore mi dia il suo nome ed indirizzo.
per fah-vo'-re mi di'-ah il su'-o no'-me ed in-di-ri'-tso.

Let me see your driver's license.
Mi mostri la sua patente di guida.
mi mos'-tri lah su'-ah pah-ten'-te di gwi'-dah.

What is the name of your insurance company?
Con quale compagnia è assicurato?
kon kwah'-le kom-pah-nyi'-ah è ahs-sı-ku-rah'-to?

How badly damaged is your car?
Quanto danno ha subito la sua vettura?
kwahn'-to dahn'-no ah su-bi'-to lah su'-ah vet-tu'-rah?

I have lost my tourist card.
Ho perduto il mio permesso di soggiorno.
ò per-du'-to il mi'-o per-mes'-so di soj-jor'-no.

Can I get a replacement?
Si può ottenere un facsimile?
si pwò ot-te-ne'-re un fahk-si'-mi-le?

What is the charge?
Quant'è la tassa?
kwahn-tè lah tahs'-sah?

I have lost a suitcase.
Ho smarrito una valigia.
ò zmahr-ri'-to u'-nah vah-li'-jah.

It carries the initials R. D. L.
Le iniziali incise sono R. D. L.
le in-ni-tsyah'-li in-chi-ze so'-no èr-re di èl-le.

If it comes in, telephone me at 54-227.
Se fosse rinvenuta, vorrebbe telefonarmi al numero 54-227.
se fos'-se rin-ve-nu'-tah, vor-rèb-be te-le-fo-nahr'-mi ahl nu'-me-ro chin'-kwe kwaht'-tro du'-e du'-e sèt-te.

THE CLOCK AND THE CALENDAR

What time is it?
Che ora è?
ke o'-rah è?

It is ten a.m.
Sono le dieci.
so'-no le dye'-chi.

It is a quarter past three p.m.
Sono le tre e quindici.
so'-no le tre e kwin'-di-chi.

It is half past seven.
Sono le sette e mezza.
so'-no le sèt-te e mè-dzah.

It is quarter to nine.
Sono le nove meno un quarto.
so'-no le nò-ve me'-no un kwahr'-to.

The days of the week are: Monday, Tuesday, Wednesday, Thursday, Friday, Saturday, Sunday.
I giorni della settimana sono: lunedì, martedì, mercoledì, giovedì, venerdì, sabato, domenica.
i jor'ni del'-lah set-ti-mah'-nah so'-no lu-ne-di', mahr-te-di', mer-ko-le-di', jo-ve-di', ve-ner-di', sah'bah-to, do-me'-ni-kah.

The months of the year are: January, February, March, April, May,
    June, July, August, September, October, November, December.
**I mesi dell'anno sono: gennaio, febbraio, marzo, aprile, maggio,
    giugno, luglio, agosto, settembre, ottobre, novembre, dicembre.**
i me'-si del-lahn'-no so'-no: jen-nah'-yo, feb-brah'-yo, mahr'-tso,
    ah-pri'-le, mahj'-jo, ju'-nyo, lu'-lyo, ah-gos'-to, set-tem'-bre,
    ot-to'-bre, no-vèm-bre, di-chèm-bre.

The seasons of the year are: Spring, Summer, Autumn, Winter.
**Le stagioni dell'anno sono: la primavera, l'estate, l'autunno,
    l'inverno.**
le stah-jo'-ni del-lahn'-no so'-no pri-mah-vè-rah, es-tah'-te,
    ah-u-tun'-no, invèr-no.

I'll be 33 years old on July 16, 1967.
**Compirò trentatre anni il diciassette luglio mille novecento
    sessantasette.**
kom-pi-rò tren-tah-tre' ahn'-ni il di-chah-sèt-te lu'-lyo mil'-le
    no-ve-chen'-to ses-sahn-tah-sèt-te.

How is the weather?	It is fine.	It is a beautiful day.
Che tempo fa?	**Fa bel tempo.**	**È una bella giornata.**
ke tèm-po fah?	*fah bèl tèm-po.*	*è u'-nah bèl-lah jor-nah'-tah.*

It is raining (snowing).   It is showering (drizzling).
Piove (nevica).   **Piove a dirotto (pioviggina).**
pyò-ve (ne'-vi-kah).   *pyò-ve ah di-rot'-to (pyo-vij'-ji-nah).*

What are the holidays in Italy?
Quali sono i giorni di feria in Italia?
kwah'-li so'-no i jor'ni di fè-ryah in i-tah'-li-ah?

New Year's Day, Easter, Christmas.
Il Capodanno, il giorno di Pasqua, il giorno di Natale.
il kah-po-dahn'-no, il jor'-no di pah'-skwah, il jor'-no di nah-tah'-le.

ABOARD SHIP

I am traveling first class. Stateroom No. 53.
Ho una cabina di prima classe. Cabina numero cinquantatre.
ò u'-nah kah-bi'-nah di pri'-mah klahs'-se. kah-bi'-nah nu'-me-ro
    chin-kwahn-tah-tre'.

Can you please direct me?
Mi scusi, può dirmi da che parte devo andare?
mi sku'-zi, pwò dir-mi dah ke pahr'-te dè-vo ahn-dah'-re?

You are on C deck.
Lei sta sul ponte C.
lè-y stah sul pon'-te "chi".

Take our bags to our cabin.
Vuol portare il nostro bagaglio in cabina?
vwòl por-tah're il nò-stro bah-gah'-lyo in kah-bi'nah?

In what direction is it?
Da che parte si trova?
dah ke pahr'-te si trò-vah?

Where is the purser's office?
Dov'è l'ufficio del commissario?
do-vè luf-fi'-cho del kom-mis-sah'-ryo?

What time is lunch served?
A che ora è servita la colazione?
ah ke o'-rah è ser-vi'-tah lah ko-lah-tsyo'-ne?

The first sitting is at twelve.
Il primo turno è a mezzogiorno.
il pri'-mo tur'-no è ah me-dzo-jor'-no.

The second at one.
Il secondo all'una (al tocco).
il se-kon'-do ahl-lu'-nah (ahl-tòk-ko).

At what time is dinner served?
A che ora si serve il pranzo?
ah ke o-rah si sèr-ve il prahn'-dzo?

Dinner is served at six.
Il pranzo si serve alle sei.
il prahn'-dzo si sèr-ve ahl'-le sè-y.

I would like to rent a deck chair.
Vorrei fissare una sedia a sdraio sul ponte.
vor-rè-y fis-sah'-re u'-nah sè-dyah ah zdrah'-yo sul pon'-te.

How much does a deck chair cost?
Quanto si paga per una sedia sul ponte?
kwahn'-to si pah'-gah per un'-ah sè-dyah sul pon'-te?

The cost is 2 dollars.
Il prezzo è di due dollari.
il prè-tso è di du'-e dòl-lah-ri.

I should like to take a bath every morning at 9.
Vorrei fare un bagno ogni mattina alle nove.
vor-rè-y fah'-re un bah'-nyo o'-nyi maht-ti'-nah ahl'-le nò-ve.

At what time does the boat dock tomorrow?
A che ora si approda domani?
ah ke o'-rah si ahp-prò-dah do-mah'-ni?

We will dock at 8:00.
Si approda alle otto.
si ahp-prò-dah ahl'-le òt-to.

PLANE TRAVEL

How do I get to the airport?
Come si va all'aeroporto?
ko'-me si vah ahl-lah-e-ro-por'-to?

When does the bus leave for the airport?
Quando parte l'autobus per l'aeroporto?
kwahn'-do pahr'-te lah'-u-to-bus per lah-e-re-por'-to?

Is there a plane for Rome?
C'è un aeroplano per Roma?
chè un ah-e-ro-plah'-no per ro'-mah?

When does it leave?
A che ora parte?
ah-ke' o'-rah pahr'-te?

How long is the flight?
Quanto tempo impiega il volo?
kwahn'-to tèm-po im-pi-è-gah il vo'-lo?

What is the fare?
Quanto costa il biglietto?
kwahn'-to kòs-tah il bi-lyet'to?

I'd like to reserve a seat on the next flight.
Vorrei riservare un posto pel prossimo volo.
vor-rè-y ri-ser-vah'-re un po'-sto pel pròs-si-mo vo'-lo.

A seat next to the window, please.
Un posto accanto al finestrino, per favore.
un po'-sto ahk-kahn'-to ahl fi-nes-tri'-no, per fah-vo'-re.

Is lunch (dinner) served on this flight?
Si serve la colazione (il pranzo) durante questo volo?
si. sèr-ve lah ko-lah-tsyo'-ne (il prahn'-dzo) du-rahn'-te kwes'-to vo'-lo?

Is my luggage carried free?
Va gratis il mio bagaglio?
vah grah'-tis il mi'-o bah-gah'-lyo?

It is five pounds overweight. You must pay 1200 lire.
Pesa cinque libbre oltre il limite. Deve pagare 1200 lire.
*pe'-zah chin'-kwe lib'-bre ol'-tre il li'-mi-te. de'-ve pah-gah'-re
mil'-le e du-e-chèn-to li'-re.*

Stewardess, I feel airsick.
Signorina, ho male d'aria.
si-nyo-ri'-nah, ò mah'-le dah'-ryah.

Do you have a remedy?
Ha un rimedio?
ah un ri-me'-dyo?

Will the plane arrive on time?
Arriverà in orario l'aeroplano?
ahr-ri-ve-rah' in o-rah'-ryo lah-e-ro-plah'-no?

TRAVEL BY RAIL

Where is the ticket office?
Dov'è l'ufficio biglietti (la biglietteria)?
do-vè luf-fi'-cho bi-lyet'-ti (lah bi-lyet-te-ri'-ah)?

One ticket to Bari.
Un biglietto per Bari.
un bi-lyet'-to per bah'-ri.

First (second) class.
Di prima (seconda) classe.
di pri'-mah (se-kon'-dah) klahs'-se.

One way.
Di andata.
di ahn-dah'-tah.

Round trip.
Di andata e ritorno.
di ahn-dah'-tah e ri-tor'-no.

What time does this train leave?
A che ora parte questo treno?
ah-ke' o'-rah pahr'-te kwes'-to trè-no?

When does it arrive?
A che ora arriverà?
ah-ke' o'-rah ahr-ri-ve-rah'?

Is it an express or a local?
E' un direttissimo o accelerato?
è un di-ret-tis'-si-mo o ah-chel-le-rah'-to?

Is this seat taken?
E' occupato questo posto?
è ok-ku-pah'-to kwes'-to pos'-to?

Is smoking permitted here?
E' permesso fumare qui?
è per-mes'-so fu-mah'-re kwi?

Tickets, please.
Biglietti, per favore.
bi-lyet'-ti, per fah-vo'-re.

The dining car is now open.
Il vagone ristorante è aperto ora.
il vah-go'-ne ris-to-rahn'-te è ah-pèr-to o'rah.

Which way is the sleeping car?
Da che parte è il vagone-letto?
dah ke pahr'-te è il vah-gò-ne lèt-to?

When is the next train for Torino?
Quando parte il prossimo treno per Torino?
kwahn'-do pahr'-te il pròs-si-mo trè-no per to-ri'-no?

GOING THROUGH CUSTOMS

Open your baggage, please.
Apra le sue valige, per favore.
ah'-prah le su'-e vah-li'-je, per fah-vo'-re.

Do you have anything besides wearing apparel?
C'è qualcosa oltre gl'indumenti personali?
chè kwahl-kò-zah ol-tre lyin-du-men'-ti per-so-nah'-li?

Yes, a few toilet articles.
Sì, alcuni articoli da toletta.
si, ahl-ku'ni ahr-ti'-ko-li dah to-let'-tah.

And my camera.
E la mia macchina fotografica.
e lah mi'-ah mahk'-ki-nah fo-to-grah'-fi-kah.

Is the camera for personal use?
E' per uso personale la macchina?
è per u'-zo per-so-nah'-le lah mahk'-ki-nah?

Yes, it is.
Sì, (lo è).
si', (lo è).

How many cigarettes do you have?
Quante sigarette ha?
kwahn'-te si-gah-ret'-te ah?

I have two cartons.
Due stecche.
du'-e stek'-ke.

That's the maximum allowed.
E' il massimo concesso.
è il mahs'-si-mo kon-chès-so.

Where are your papers, please?
Mi mostri i suoi documenti, per favore.
mi mo'-stri i swo'-i do-cu-men'-ti, per fah-vo'-re.

I hope you have a nice stay with us.
Le auguro felice soggiorno.
le ah-u'-gu-ro fe-li'-ce soj-jor'-no.

Will you call a porter, please?
Vuole chiamarmi un portabagagli, per favore?
vwò-le kyah-mahr'-mi un por-tah-bah-gah'-lyi, per fah-vo'-re?

Porter, please take my bags.
Portabagagli, porti le mie valige.
por-tah-bah-gah'-lyi, por'-ti le mi'-e vah-li'-je.

To the taxi stand.
Al posteggio tassì.
ahl pos-tej'-jo tahs-si'.

To the bus station.
Alla fermata autobus.
ah'-lah fer-mah'-tah ah-ú-to-bus.

How much do you charge?
Quánto mi farà pagare?
kwahn'-to mi fah-rah'-pah-gah'-re?

That is too much.
E' troppo.
è tròp-po.

I will pay you 500 lire.
Le darò cinquecento lire.
le dah-rò chin-kwe-chèn-to li'-re.

Follow me please.
Mi segua, per favore.
mi se'-gwah, per fah-vo'-re.

TAXI!

Taxi.
Tassì!
Tahs-si'!

I'm in a hurry.
Ho fretta.
ò fret'-tah.

Take me to the shopping center.
Mi conduca al quartiere dei magazzini (al centro).
mi kon-du'-kah ahl kwahr-tye'-re de'-y mah-gah-dzi'-ni (ahl chèn-tro).

What's this building on the right (on the left)?
Che palazzo è quello a destra (a sinistra)?
ke pah-lah'-tso è kwel'-lo ah des'-trah (ah si-nis'-trah)?

Please don't drive so fast.
Per favore, non corra tanto.
per fah-vo'-re, non kor'-rah tahn'-to.

Stop at the corner.
Si fermi all'angolo.
si fer'-mi ahl-lahn'-go-lo.

What's the charge?
Quanto devo? (Quanto fa?)
kwahn'-to dè-vo? (kwahn'-to fah?)

BUS STOP

Where is the bus stop?
Dov'è la fermata autobus?
do-vè lah fer-mah'-tah ah-u'-to-bus?

Does the bus to Padova stop here?
Si ferma qui l'autobus per Padova?
si fer'-mah kwi lah-u'-to-bus per pah'-do-vah?

How often do the buses run?
Con che frequenza passano gli autobus?
kon ke fre-kwèn-tsah pahs'-sah-no lyi ah-u'-to-bus?

When is the next bus to Parma?
Quando parte il prossimo autobus per Parma?
kwanh'-do pahr'-te il pròs-si-mo ah'-u-to-bus per pahr'-mah?

How much is the fare?
Quanto costa la corsa?
kwahn'-to kòs-tah lah kor'-sah?

Please let me know when we reach Siena.
Favorisca avvisarmi quando si arriva a Siena.
fah-vo-ris'-kah ahv-vi-zahr'-mi kwahn'-do si ahr-ri'-vah ah sie-nah.

Driver, please let me off.
Conducente, mi faccia scendere.
kon-du-chèn-te, mi fah'-chah shen'-de-re.

How late do the buses run on this line?
Fino a che ora c'è servizio su questa linea?
fi'-no ah ke o'-rah chè ser-vi'-tsyo su kwes'-tah li'-ne-ah?

MOTORING THROUGH ITALY

Where is the nearest gas station?
Dov'è il rifornimento benzina più vicino?
do-vè il ri-for-ni-men'-to ben-dzi'-nah pyu vi-chi'-no?

Give me 20 liters of gas.
Mi dia venti litri di benzina.
mi di'-ah ven'-ti li'tri di ben-dzi'-nah.

Fill 'er up (Fill the tank).
Riempia il serbatoio.
ri-em'pyah il ser-bah-to'-yo

A liter of oil.
Un litro d'olio.
un li'-tro dò-lyo.

Check the oil, water and battery.
Controlli l'olio, l'acqua e la batteria.
kon-trol'-li lò-lyo, lahk'-kwah e lah baht-te-ri'-ah.

Please check my tires.
Per favore, verifichi i pneumatici (le gomme).
per fah-vo'-re, ve-ri'-fi-ki i pne-u-mah'-ti-chi (le gom'-me).

Is this the road to Milano?
E' questa la strada per andare a Milano?
è kwes'-tah lah strah'-dah per ahn-dah'-re ah mi-lah'-no?

Straight ahead 15 kilometers.
Avanti diritto quindici chilometri.
ah-vahn'-ti di-rit'-to kwin'-di-chi ki-lò-me-tri.

Turn left (right) at the next crossroad.
Giri a sinistra (a destra) al prossimo crocevia.
ji'-ri ah si-nis'-trah (ah des'-trah) ahl pròs-si-mo kro-che-vi'-ah.

There is a detour 4 kilometers from here.
C'è una deviazione a quattro chilometri di qui.
chè u'-nah de-vyah-tsyo'-ne ah kwaht'-tro ki-lò-me-tri di kwi.

Can we reach Naples before night fall?
Si può arrivare a Napoli prima che imbrunisca?
si pwò ahr-ri-vah'-re ah nah'-po-li pri'-mah ke im-bru-nis'-kah?

What town is this?
Che cittadina è questa?
e chit-tah-di'-nah è kwes'-tah?

Where does this road go?
Dove porta questa strada?
do'-ve por'-tah kwes'-tah strah'-dah?

I have a flat tire.
Ho una gomma forata (Ho un pneumatico forato).
u'nah gom'-mah fo-rah'-tah (ò un pne-u-mah'-ti-ko fo-rah'-to).

My headlights don't work.
I fanali non funzionano.
fah-nah'-li non fun-tsyo'-nah-no.

Where is a service station?
Dov'è una stazione di servizio?
o-vè u'-nah stah-tsyo'-ne di ser-vi'-tsyo?

May I have some water for my car please?
Posso avere acqua per l'automobile?
òs-so ah-ve'-re ahk'-kwah per lah-u-to-mò-bi-le?

Can you give my car a push?
Può dare una spinta alla mia automobile?
wò dah'-re u'-nah spin'-tah ahl-lah mi'-ah ah-u-to-mò-bi-le?

Can you give me a lift to Palermo?
Può darmi un passaggio a Palermo?
wò dahr'-mi pahs-sahj'-jo ah pah-lèr-mo?

AUTO PARTS

Accelerator.	Acceleratore.	*(ah-che-le-rah-to'-re)*
Battery.	Batteria.	*(baht-te-ri'-ah)*
Bolt.	Bullone.	*(bul-lo'-ne)*
Brake.	Freni.	*(fre'-ni)*
Bumper.	Paraurti.	*(pah-rah-ur'-ti)*
Cable.	Cavo.	*(kah'-vo)*
Chains.	Catene.	*(kah-te'-ne)*
Clutch.	Frizione.	*(fri-tsyo'-ne)*
Door handle.	Maniglia.	*(mah-ni'-lyah)*
Engine.	Motore.	*(mo-to'-re)*
Fender.	Parafango.	*(pah-rah-fahn'-go)*
Gear shift.	Leva del cambio.	*(lè-vah del kahm'-byo)*
Hammer.	Martello.	*(mahr-tèl-lo)*

Headlight.	**Faro.**	*(fah'-ro)*
Hood.	**Cofano.**	*(kò-fah-no)*
Horn.	**Clacson.**	*(klahk'-son)*
Ignition.	**Accensione.**	*(ah-chen-syo'-ne)*
Jack.	**Cricco.**	*(krik'-ko)*
Key.	**Chiave.**	*(kyah'-ve)*
Nut.	**Dado.**	*(dah'-do)*
Pliers.	**Pinze.**	*(pin'-dze)*
Rope.	**Fune.**	*(fu'-ne)*
Screwdriver.	**Cacciavite.**	*(kah-char-vi'-te)*
Spark plugs.	**Candele.**	*(kahn-de'-le)*
Spring.	**Molla.**	*(mol-lah)*
Starter.	**Avviamento.**	*(ahv-vya-men'-to)*
Steering wheel.	**Volante.**	*(vo-lahn'-te)*
Tire.	**Pneumatico.**	*(pne-u-mah'-ti-co)*
Wheel.	**Ruota.**	*(rwo'-tah)*
Windshield wiper.	**Tergicristallo.**	*(ter-ji-kris-tahl'-lo)*
Wrench.	**Chiave inglese.**	*(kyah'-ve in-gle'-ze)*

AT THE HOTEL

I made a reservation by letter (by phone).
Ho fatta una prenotazione per lettera (per telefono).
ò faht'-to u'-nah pre-no-tah-tsyo'-ne per lèt-te-rah (per te-lè-fo-no).

Do you have a room with a double bed (twin beds)?
Ha una camera con letto matrimoniale (con due letti)?
*ah u'-nah kah'-me-rah kon let'-to mah-tri-mo-nyah'-le
        (kon du'-e lèt-ti)?*

Does the room have a bath?
È una camera con bagno?
è u'-nah kah'-me-rah kon bah'-nyo?

I want a room without bath.
Voglio una camera senza bagno.
vo'-lyo u'-nah kah'-me-rah sèn-tsah bah'-nyo.

What is the price of this room?
Qual'è il prezzo di questa camera?
kwahl-lè il prè-tso di kwes'-tah kah'-me-rah?

How long are you planning to stay?
Per quanto tempo intende fermarsi?
per kwahn'-to tèm'-po in-tèn-de fer-mahr'-si?

I am planning to stay 7 days.
Ho intenzione di rimanere sette giorni.
ò in-ten-tsyo'-ne di ri-mah-ne'-re sèt-te jor'-ni.

The price for a single day is 1,500 lire.
Per un giorno solo, il prezzo è di mille e cinquecento lire.
per un jor'-no so'-lo il prè-tso è di mil'-le e chin-kwe-chèn-to li'-re.

For a week we have a special rate of 8,000 lire.
Per una settimana c'è una riduzione, costerebbe ottomila lire.
*per u'-nah set-ti-mah'-nah chè u'-nah ri-du-tsyo'-ne, kos-te-rèb-be
    òt-to-mi-lah li'-re.*

Does that include service and tax?　　Are meals included?
Incluso il servizio e le tasse?　　**Sono inclusi i pasti?**
in-klu'-zo il ser-vi'-tsyo e le tahs'-se?　　*so'-no in-klu'-zi i pah'-sti?*

Do you have something less expensive?
Ha qualche cosa meno cara?
ah kwahl'-ke kò-zah me'-no kah'-rah?

I want a smaller (larger) room.
Vorrei una camera più piccola (grande).
vor-rè-y u'-nah kah'-me-rah pyu pik'-ko-lah (grahn'-de).

Yes, this room will do.　　What is the price?
Sì, questa camera va bene.　　**Quanto costa?**
si, kwes'-tah kah'-me-rah vah bè-ne.　　*kwahn'-to kò-stah?*

Please have my bags carried up.
Per favore, faccia portar su le mie valige.
per fah-vo'-re, fah'-chah por-tahr' su le mi'-e vah-li'-je.

Will you register, please?
Per favore, mi dia le sue generalità.
per fah-vo'-re, mi di'-ah le su'-e je-ne-rah-li-tah'.

I would like to check my valuables in your safe.
Vorrei depositare i miei valori.
vor-rè-y de-po-zi-tah'-re i myè-y vah-lo'-ri.

Please let me have the key to my room.
Vuole darmi la chiave della mia camera?
vwòl dahr'-mi lah kyah'-ve del'-lah mi'-ah kah'-me-rah?

Is there a washroom on the floor?
C'è un lavatoio a questo piano?
chè un lah-vah-to'-yo ah kwes'-to pyah'-no?

Where is the bathroom?
Dov'è la stanza da bagno?
do-vè lah stahn'-tsah dah bah'-nyo?

I am expecting a visitor.
Sto in attesa di una visita.
sto in aht-te'-zah di u'-nah vi'-zi-tah.

Will you please ask him to wait in the lobby?
Per favore gli chieda la cortesia d'aspettare nel salone.
per fah-vo'-re lyi kye'-dah lah kor-te-zi'-ah dah-spet-tah'-re nel sah-lo'-ne.

I am planning to leave tomorrow.
Intendo partire domani..
in-ten'-do pahr-ti'-re do-mah'-ni.

I am going on a trip to Capri.
Faccio un viaggetto a Capri.
fah'-cho un vyahj-jet'-to ah kah'-pri.

May I leave some of my baggage here?
Posso lasciare qui parte del mio bagaglio?
pòs-so lah-shah'-re kwi pahr'-te del mi'-o bah-gah'-lyo?

I will be back on Monday.
Sarò di ritorno lunedì.
sah-rò di ri-tor'-no lu-ne-di'.

Please have my bill ready.
Per favore, faccia preparare il conto.
per fah-vo'-re, fah'-chah pre-pah-rah'-re il kon'-to.

Please send a boy for my bags.
Per favore, mandi qualcuno a prendere le valige.
per fah-vo'-re, mahn'-di kwahl-ku'-no ah prèn-de-re le vah-li'-je.

Have my bags taken to the station.
Faccia portare le valige alla stazione.
fah'-chah por-tah'-re le vah-li'-je ahl'-lah stah-tsyo'ne.

Would you have a taxi ready for me.
Per favore, faccia che un tassì mi stia ad aspettare.
per fah-vo'-re, fah'-chah ke un tahs-si' mi sti'-ah ahd ahs-pet-tah'-re.

Kindly call a taxi.
Per favore, mi chiami un tassì.
per fah-vo'-re mi kyah'-mi' un tahs-si'.

We enjoyed our stay here very much.
Siamo molto contenti del soggiorno qui.
syah'-mo mol'-to kon-tèn-ti del soj-jor'-no kwi.

RENTING A ROOM

Do you want a furnished or unfurnished room?
Desidera una camera mobiliata o vuota?
de-zi'-de-rah u'-nah kah'-me-rah mo-bi-lyah'-tah o vwò-tah?

I want a furnished room with (without) bath and breakfast.
Desidero una camera mobiliata con (senza) bagno e la prima colazione.
de-zi'-de-ro u'-nah kah'-me-rah mo-bi-lyah'-tah kon (sen'-tsah)
    bah'-nyo e lah pri'-mah ko-lah-tsyo'-ne.

I will eat my noon meal elsewhere.
Farò la seconda colazione altrove.
fah-rò lah se-kon'-dah ko-lah-tsyo'-ne ahl-tro'-ve.

Would you prefer a room which looks out on the street or on the sea?
Preferisce una camera che dia sulla strada o sul mare?
pre-fe-ri'-she u'-nah kah'-me-rah ke di'-ah sul'-lah strah'-dah o
    sul mah'-re?

I shall take the one with the view of the sea.
Prenderò quella che dà sul mare.
pren-de-rò kwel'-lah ke dah sul mah'-re.

What price will you charge, including tax and service?
Quanto è, inclusi servizio e tassa?
kwahn'-to è in-klu'-zi ser-vi'-tsyo e tahs'-sah?

Could you give me a slightly lower price?
Me la può dare per meno?
me lah pwò dah'-re per me'-no?

After all, I will be here 6 weeks.
Consideri che rimarrò qui sei settimane.
kon-si'-de-ri ke ri-mahr-rò kwi sè-y set-ti-mah'-ne.

I wish to take a bath.
Vorrei fare un bagno.
vor-rè-y fah'-re un bah'-nyo.

Let me know when it is ready.
Vuol avvertirmi quando sarà pronto?
vwòl ahv-ver-tir'-mi kwahn'-do sah-rah' pron'-to?

Bring me some more coat-hangers.
Mi porti delle grucce di più, per favore.
mi por'-ti del'-le gru'-che di pyu, per fah-vo'-re?

Would you press a dress?
Può farmi stirare un vestito?
pwò fahr'-mi sti-rah'-re un ves-ti'-to?

I will need it back at seven o'clock.
Lo desidero di ritorno per le sette.
lo de-zi'-de-ro di ri-tor'-no per le sèt-te.

I wish to be called at seven o'clock.
Per favore, mi faccia svegliare alle sette.
per fah-vo'-re, mi fah'-chah zve-lyah'-re ahl'-le sèt-te.

Have breakfast sent up at 8.
Per favore, mi faccia servire la colazione in camera alle otto.
per fah-vo're, mi fah'-chah ser-vi'-re lah ko-lah-tsyo'-ne in kah'-me-rah ahl'-le òt-to.

I wish to have coffee and rolls.
Desidero caffè e panini.
de-zi'-de-ro kahf-fè e pah-ni'-ni.

Where is the dining room?
Dov'è la sala da pranzo?
do-vè lah sah'-lah dah prahn'-dzo?

Take all messages.
Prenda tutti i messaggi.
pren'-dah tut'-ti i mes-sah'-ji.

And look after my mail.
E si occupi della mia posta.
e si ok'-ku-pi del'-lah mi'-ah po'-stah.

If friends call, (do not) show them to my apartment.
Se vengono degli amici, (non) li faccia salire.
se ven'-go-no del'-yi ah-mi'-chi (non) li fah'-chah sah-li'-re.

THE SIDEWALK CAFE

Waiter!
Cameriere!
kah-me-ryè-re!

A beer, please.
Una birra, per favore.
u'-nah bir'-rah, per fah-vo'-re.

A Scotch whisky.
Un whisky scozzese.
un whi-ski sko-tse'-se.

What fruit juices do you have?
Che succo di frutta può darmi?
ke suk'-ko di frut'-tah pwò dahr'-mi?

We have orange, tomato and grapefruit.
Abbiamo succo d'arancia, di pomodoro e di pompelmo.
ahb-byah'-mo suk'-ko dah-rahn'-chah, di-po-mo-dò-ro e di pom-pel'-mo.

A glass of sherry.
Un bicchiere di vino sceri.
un bik-kyè-re di vi'-no she'-ri.

What kind of liqueurs do you have?
Che tipo di liquore si può avere?
ke ti'-po di li-kwo'-re si pwò ah-ve'-re?

A glass of red (white) wine.
Un bicchiere di vino rosso (bianco).
un bik-kyè-re di vi'-no ros'-so (byahn'-ko).

The check, please.
Il conto, per favore.
il kon'-to, per fah-vo'-re.

Is the service included?
E' incluso il servizio?
è in-klu'-zo il ser-vi'-tsyo?

No, it is not.
No, non è incluso.
no, non è in-klu'-zo.

DINING OUT

Can you recommend a good restaurant?
Mi può raccomandare un buon ristorante (una buona trattoria)?
*mi pwò rahk-ko-mahn-dah-re un bwòn ri-sto-rahn'-te
(u'-nah bwo'-nah traht-to-ri'-ah)?*

I would like to reserve a table for 7 o'clock.
Vorrei prenotare una tavola per le sette.
vor-rè-y pre-no-tah'-re u'-nah tah'-vo-lah per le sèt-te.

A table for two, please.
Una tavola per due, per piacere.
u'-nah tah'-vo-lah per du'-e, per pyah-che'-re.

Do you serve a la carte or table d'hôte?
Si serve un pasto fisso o si può ordinare a volontà?
si sèr-ve un pahs'-to fis'-so o si pwò or-di-nah'-re ah vo-lon-tah'?

May I have a menu, please?
Vuol darmi il menù (la lista)?
vwòl dahr'-mi il me-nu' (lah li'-stah)?

What is the specialty of the house?
Qual'è la specialità della casa?
kuah-lè lah spe-chah-li-tah' del-lah kah'-zah?

What does this dish consist of?
Di che consiste questo piatto?
di ke kon-si'-ste kwe'-sto pyaht'-to?

What do you recommend?
Che cosa raccomanda lei?
ke kò-zah rahk-ko-mahn'-dah le'-y?

I suggest that you eat manicotti.
Le suggerisco prendere dei manicotti.
le suj-je-ris'-ko prèn-de-re de'-y mah-ni-kot'-ti.

Please suggest something simpler and less expensive.
Mi suggerisca qualche cosa più semplice e meno cara.
mi suj-je-ris'-kah kwahl'-ke ko'-zah pyu sem'-pli-che e mè-no kah'-rah.

Bring me a pitcher of ice water.
Mi porti una brocca d'acqua fresca, per favore.
mi pòr-ti u'-nah bròk-kah dah'-kwah fres'-kah, per fah-vo'-re.

A glass of plain water, please.
Un bicchiere d'acqua, per piacere.
un bik-kye'-re dah'-kwah,
        per pyah-che'-re.

I will start with ravioli.
Comincerò con dei ravioli.
ko-min-che-rò kon de'-y rah-vyo'-li.

My wife will have lasagna.
Mia moglie prenderà una lasagna.
mi'-ah mo'-lye pren-de-rah' u'-nah lah-zah'-nyah.

For soup we will have minestrone.
Per prima portata mi dia un minestrone.
per pri'-mah por-tah'-tah mi di'-ah un mi-nes-trò-ne.

For the main course I would like saltimbocca.
Per il piatto forte vorrei dei saltimbocca.
per il pyaht'-to fòr-te vor-rè-y de'-y sahl-tim-bòk-kah.

Please serve us quickly. We are in a hurry.
Per favore, ci serva presto. Abbiamo fretta.
per fah-vo're, chi sèr-vah prè-sto. ahb-byah'-mo fret'-tah.

Would you like something to drink, sir?
Vorrebbe qualche cosa da bere, signore?
vor-rèb-be kwahl'-ke kò-zah dah be'-re, si-nyo'-re?

May I see the wine list.
Vuol mostrarmi la lista dei vini?
vwòl mo-strahr'-mi lah li'-stah de'-y vi'-ni?

Which wine goes with this dish?
Che vino va con questo piatto?
ke vi'-no vah kon kwe'-sto pyaht'-to?

A half carafe of ordinary red wine.
Mezzo litro di vino rosso.
med'-dzo li'-tro di vi'-no ros'-so.

Bring me a glass of local wine.
Mi porti un bicchiere di vino di questa regione.
mi pòr-ti un bik-kyè-re di vi'-no di kwe'-stah re-jo'-ne.

The wine seems to be a bit sour.
Pare che il vino dia un po' all'acido.
pah'-re ke il vi'-no di'-ah un pò ahl-lah'-chi-do.

Waiter, you forgot to give me a napkin.
Cameriere, ha dimenticato di darmi un tovagliolo (una salvietta).
*kah-me-ryè-re ah di-men-ti-kah'-to di dahr'-mi un to-vah-lyò-lo
    (u'-nah sahl-vyet'-tah).*

Some bread, please.
Del pane, per favore.
del pah'-ne, per fah-vo'-re.

Do you have any rolls?
Può darmi dei panini?
pwò dahr'-mi de'-y pah-ni'-ni?

More butter.
Un pò più di burro.
un pò pyu di bur'ro.

Let me have a tart for dessert.
Per dolce, mi dia un pasticciotto.
per dol'-che mi di'-ah un pahs-tich-chòt-to.

Waiter, the check please.
Cameriere, il conto per favore.
kah-mer-yè-re, il kon'-to per fah-vo'-re.

I think you've added up this bill incorrectly.
Mi pare che la somma non sia giusta.
mi pah'-re ke lah som'-mah non si'-ah ju'-stah.

I'll check it again.
Rifarò l'addizione.
ri-fah-rò lahd-di-tsyo'-ne.

You are right; I've made a mistake.
Ha ragione; ho fatto un errore.
ah rah-jo'-ne; ò faht'- to un er-ro'-re.

We enjoyed the meal very much.
Abbiamo gustato molto il pranzo.
ahb-byah'-mo gu-stah'-to mol'-to il'prahn'-dzo.

We'll be glad to recommend this place to our friends.
Vi raccomanderemo con piacere ai nostri amici.
vi rahk-ko-mahn-de-re'-mo kon pyah-che'-re' ah'-y no'-stri ah-mi'-chi.

The service was excellent.
Il servizio è stato eccellente.
il ser-vi'-tsyo è stah-to e-chel-lèn-te.

ITALIAN FOODS

Breakfast.	Lunch.
Prima colazione.	**Seconda colazione (merenda).**
pri'-mah ko-lah-tsyo'-ne.	*se-kon'-dah ko-lah-tsyo'-ne (me-rèn-dah).*

Dinner.	Supper.	Snack.
Pranzo.	**Cena.**	**Spuntino.**
prahn'-dzo.	*che'-nah.*	*spun-ti'-no.*

Orange juice (grapefruit, tomato).
Succo d'arancia (di pompelmo, di pomodori).
suk'-ko dah-rahn'-chah (di pom-pèl-mo, di po-mo-dò-ri).

Two soft-boiled eggs (hard boiled, scrambled, poached, fried).
Due uova a bere (sode, strapazzate, affogate, fritte).
du'e uò-vah ah be'-re (sò-de, strah-pah-tsah'-te, ahf-fo-gah'-te, frit'-te).

Ham and eggs (bacon).
Due uova con prosciutto (con pancetta).
du'-e uò-vah kon pro-shut'-to (kon pahn-chet'-tah).

Toast and butter (jam).
Pane abbrustolito (tostato) con burro (marmellata).
pah'-ne ahb-bru-sto-li'-to (to-stah'-to) kon bur'-ro (mahr-mel-lah'-tah).

Coffee with milk.
Caffè latte.
kahf-fè laht'-te.

Tea with lemon.	Sugar.
Tè con limone.	**Zucchero.**
tè kon li-mo'-ne.	*tsuk'-ke-ro.*

Another cup of coffee, please.
Un'altra tazza di caffè, per favore.
unahl'-trah tah'-tsah di kahf-fè, per fah-vo'-re.

Soup (noodle, lentil, consomme, chicken).
Brodo (con pastina, di lenticchie, ristretto, di pollo).
brò-do (kon pah-sti'-nah, di len-tik'-kye, ri-stret'-to, di pol'-lo).

Hors d'oeuvre.
Antipasto.
ahn-ti-pah'-sto.

A glass of water.
Un bicchiere d'acqua.
un bik-kyè-re dah'-kwah.

A fresh vegetable salad (with mayonnaise; with oil and vinegar).
Un'insalata di verdure (con mayonnaise; con olio e aceto).
*un in-sah-lah'-tah di ver-du'-re (kon mah-yo-nè-se;
          kon o'-lyo e ah-che'-to).*

Small fried pieces of veal with Marsala wine sauce.
Scaloppine al Marsala.
skah-lohp-pi'-ne ahl mahr-sah'-lah.

Cutlet with mozzarella and tomato sauce.
Cotoletta alla parmigiana.
ko-to-let'-tah ah'-lah pahr-mi-jah'-nah.

Chicken alla cacciatora.
Pollo alla cacciatora.
pòl-lo ahl'-lah kah-chah-tò-rah.

Omelette (mushroom, tomato, cheese).
Frittata avvoltolata (di funghi, di pomodori, di formaggio).
*frit-tah'-tah ahv-vol-to-lah'-tah (di fun'-gi, di po-mo-do'-ri,
          di for-mahj'-jo).*

Steak (well done, medium, rare).
Bistecca (ben cotta, a mezza cottura, al sangue).
bis-tèk-kah (bèn kot'-tah, ah me'-dzah kot-tu'-rah, ahl sahn'-gwe).

Chops (lamb, veal, pork).
Costolette (d'agnello, di vitello, di maiale).
kos-to-let'-te (dah-nyèl-lo, di vi-tel'-lo, di mah-yah'-le).

Meat loaf.
Polpettone.
pol-pet-to'-ne.

Roast veal.
Arrosto di vitello.
ahr-rò-sto di vi-tèl-lo.

Roast chicken (turkey).
Pollo arrosto (tacchino).
pol'-lo ahr-rò-sto (tahk-ki'-no).

Roast beef.
Rosbif.
roz-bif'.

Broiled steak.
Bistecca ai ferri.
bis-tèk-kah ah'-i fèr-ri.

Rolled beef.
Braciola di manzo.
brah-chò-lah di mahn'-dzo.

Stew (beef, lamb, veal)
Stufato (spezzato) (di manzo, d'agnello, di vitello).
stu-fah'-to (spe-tsah'-to) (di mahn'-dzo, dah-nyèl-lo, di vi-tèl-lo).

Sausage.
Salsiccia.
sahl-si'-chah.

Pizza (Pie).
Pizza.
pi'-tsah.

Chicken livers (with mushrooms).
Fegatini di pollo (con funghi).
fe-gah-ti'-ni di pol'-lo (kon fun'-gi).

Rice with a sauce of saffron, chicken livers and mushrooms.
Risotto alla milanese.
ri-zot'-to ahl'-lah mi-lah-ne'-ze.

Fish (broiled, fried, boiled).
Pesce (ai ferri, fritto, bollito).
pe'-she (ah'-y fèr-ri, frit'-to, bol-li'-to).

whiting	mullet (red)	bass	flounder
merluzzo	**triglia (di scoglio)**	**spigola**	**sogliola**
mer-lut'-tso	*tri'-lyah (di skò-lyo)*	*spi'-go-lah*	*sò-lyo-lah*

lobster	shrimp	squid
aragosta	**gamberi**	**calamaro, polipo**
ah-rah-go'-stah	*gahm-be'-ri*	*kah-lah-mah'-ro, pò-li-po*

Potatoes (boiled, mashed, baked, fried)
Patate (bollite, purè, al forno, fritte)
pah-tah'-te (bol-li'-te, pu-rè, ahl for'-no, frit'-te)

Vegetables.
Legumi.
le-gu'-mi.

stringbeans	peas	spinach	carrots
fagiolini	**pisellini**	**spinaci**	**carote**
fah-jo-li'-ni	*pi-zel-li'-ni*	*spi-nah'-chi*	*kah-rò-te*

broccoli	cauliflower	cabbage	squash
broccoli	**cavolfiore**	**verza**	**zucchini**
bròk-ko-li	*kah-vol-fyo'-re*	*ver'-dzah*	*tsuk-ki'-ni*

eggplant	asparagus	tomatoes	lettuce
melanzana	**asparagi**	**pomodori**	**lattuga**
me-lahn-tsah'-nah	*ahs-pah'-rah-ji*	*po-mo-dò-ri*	*laht-tu'-gah*

endives	celery	peppers	artichokes
cicorie	**sedano**	**peperoni**	**carciofi**
chi-kò-rye	*sè-dah-no*	*pe-pe-ro'-ni*	*kahr-chò-fi*

cheeses (mild)
formaggi (blandi)
for-mahj'-ji (blahn'-di)

provola	**ricotta**	**mozzarella**	**parmigiano**
prò-vo-lah	*ri-kòt-tah*	*mo-tsah-rèl-lah*	*pahr-mi-jah'-no*

(strong)
(piccanti)
pik-kahn'-ti

caciocavallo	**provolone**	**gorgonzola**
kah-cho-kah-vahl'-lo	*pro-vo-lo'-ne*	*gor-gon-zò-lah*

stracchino	**pecorino**	**svizzero**
strahk-ki'-no	*pe-ko-ri'-no*	*zvi'-tse-ro*

fruits
frutta
frut-tah

pear	apple	orange	peach	plum
pera	**mela**	**arancia**	**pesca**	**susina**
pe'-rah	*me'-lah*	*ah-rahn'-chah*	*pè'skah*	*su-zi'-nah*

cherries	apricot	tangerine	grapes	watermelon
ciliege	**albicocca**	**mandarino**	**uva**	**cocomero**
chi-lyè-je	*ahl-bi-kòk-kah*	*mahn-dah-ri'-no*	*u'-vah*	*ko-ko'-me-ro*

melon	strawberries	banana	pineapple
mellone	**fragole**	**banana**	**ananasso**
mel-lo'-ne	*frah'-go-le*	*bah-nah'-nah*	*ah-nah-nahs'-so*

figs	walnuts	almonds
fichi	**noci**	**mandorle**
fi'-ki	*no'-chi*	*mahn'-dor-le*

wine (dry, sweet, sparkling, red, white)
vino (asciutto, dolce, spumante, rosso, bianco)
vi-no (ah-shut'-to, dol'-che-spu-mahn'-te, ros'-so, byank'-ko)

mineral water	cordial, liqueur
acqua minerale	**cordiale, liquore**
ahk-kwah mi-ne-rah'-le	*kor-dyah'-le, li-kwo'-re*

ice cream	pie	pastry
gelato	**torta**	**pasticceria**
je-lah-to	*tòr-tah*	*pah-sti-che-ri'-ah*

SIGHTSEEING

I have 3 days to spend here.
Ho da passare tre giorni qui.
ò dah pahs-sah'-re tre jor'-ni kwi.

I would like to see the cathedral.
Vorrei visitare la cattedrale.
vor-rè-y vi-si-tah'-re lah kaht-te-drah'-le.

I also want to see some historical sites.
Vorrei anche vedere alcuni luòghi d'interesse storico.
vor-rè-y ahn'-ke ve-dè-re ahl-ku'-ni lwò-gi din-te-rès-se stò-ri-ko.

Tomorrow, I want to see the night life.
Domani vorrei visitare dei locali notturni.
do-mah'-ni vor-rè-y vi-si-tah'-re dè-y lo-kah'-li not-tur'-ni.

Don't send me to any expensive places.
Non mi mandi a locali troppo cari.
non mi mahn'-di ah lo-kah'-li tròp-po kah'-ri.

Here are a few I want to see.
Ecco alcuni che voglio visitare.
èk-ko ahl-ku'-ni ke vò-lyo vi-zi-tah'-re.

Can we make a tour of these places?
Si può fare un giro di questi locali?
si pwò fah-re un ji'-ro di kwe'-sti lo-kah'-li?

Are there any other interesting places?
Ci sono altri locali interessanti?
chi so'-no ahl'tri lo-kah'-li in-te-res-sahn'-ti?

I want to see the most important things.
Vorrei vedere le cose più importanti.
vor-rè-y ve-de'-re le kò-se pyu im-por-tahn'-ti.

And the market places.
Ed anche i mercati.
ed ahn'-ke i mer-kah'-ti.

I want to spend more time here.
Qui vorrei indugiare di più.
kwi vor-rè-y in-du-jah'-re di pyu.

I think I've seen enough; I am tired.
Credo di aver visto abbastanza; sono stanca.
kre'-do di ah-ver' vis'-to ahb-bah-stahn'-tsah; so'-no stahn-kah.

I would like to return to my hotel.
Vorrei rientrare in albergo.
vor-rè-y ri-en-trah'-re in ahl-ber'-go.

PHOTOGRAPHY

Would you mind letting me take your picture?
Sarebbe disposto a farmi prendere un'istantanea?
sah-rèb-be di-spò-sto ah fahr'-mi prèn-de-re un'i-stahn-tah'-ne-ah?

Just continue your work.
Continui pure a lavorare.
kon-ti'-nwi pu'-re ah lah-vo-rah'-re.

Don't look into the camera.
Non guardi l'obbiettivo.
non gwahr'-di lob-byet-ti'-vo.

Turn this way, please.
Si giri da questa parte, per favore.
si ji'-ri dah kwe'-stah pahr'-te, per fah-vo'-re.

Thank you very much for your trouble.
Mille grazie del disturbo.
mil'-le grah'-tsye del di-stur'-bo.

I would like a roll of film, number 8.
Vorrei un rollino (rotolo) di film numero otto.
vor-rè-y un rol-li'-no (rò-to-lo) di film nu'-me-ro òt-to.

Do you have color film?
Ha delle pellicole a colori?
ah del'-le pel-li'-ko-le ah ko-lo'-ri?

The shutter is stuck. Will you please look at it?
Si è incantato l'otturatore. Vuol aggiustarlo?
si è in-kahn-tah'-to lot-tu-rah-to'-re. vwòl ah-ju-stahr'-lo?

Why does my film get scratched?
Perchè si striano le pellicole?
per-kè si stri'-ah-no le pel-li'-ko-le?

Do you think I should use a filter?
Crede che dovrei usare un filtro?
kre'-de ke dov-rè-y u-zah'-re un fil'-tro?

Please develop this roll.
Per piacere, sviluppi questo ròtolo.
per pyah-che'-re, zvi-lup'-pi kwe'-sto rò-to-lo.

Please make one print of each negative.
Faccia una copia per ciascuna negativa.
fah'chah u'-nah kò-pyah per chyah-sku'-nah ne-gah-ti'-vah.

When will they be ready?
Quando saranno pronte?
kwahn'-do sah-rahn'-no pron'-te?

Do you sell flashbulbs?
Si vendono qui lampadine al magnesio?
si ven'-do-no kwi lahm-pah-di'-ne ahl mah-nyè-zyo?

Do you have 16 mm. movie film?
Ha delle pellicole cinematografiche di sedici millimetri?
ah del'-le pel-li'-ko-le chi-ne-mah-to-grah'-fi-ke di sè-di-chi mil-li'-me-tri?

SHOPPING

Where are the main department stores?
Dove si trovano i magazzini più grandi?
do've si tro'-vah-no i mah-gah-dzi'-ni pyu grahn'-di?

Is it too far to walk?
È troppo lontano per andarci a piedi?
è tròp-po lon-tah'-no per ahn-dahr'-chi ah pyè-di?

What number bus will take me there?
Con quale autobus posso andarci?
kon kwah'-le ah-u'-to-bus pòs-so ahn-dahr'-chi?

Good morning. May I look at your merchandise?
Buon giorno. È permesso dare uno sguardo alla sua merce?
*bwòn jor'-no. è per-mes'-so dah'-re u'-no zguahr'-do
    ahl'-lah su'-ah mer'-che?*

You have some nice things for sale.
Ci sono delle belle cose in vendita.
chi so'-no del'-le bel'-le kò-ze in ven'-di-tah.

I would like to see a dress (suit, skirt, blouse, slip, nightgown,
        gloves, hat).
**Vorrebbe mostrarmi un vestito (un'abito, una gonna, una blusa,
        una sottoveste, una camicia da notte, dei guanti, un cappello).**
*vor-rèb-be mo-strahr'-mi un ve-sti'-to (un ah'-bito, u'-nah gon'-nah,
        u'-nah blu-zah, u'-nah sot-to-vè-ste, u'-nah kah-mi'-chah
        dah not'-te, de'-y guahn'-ti, un kahp-pel'-lo).*

In America, I wear size 12.
Negli Stati Uniti indosso misura numero dodici.
ne'-lyi stah'-ti u-ni'-ti in-dos'-so mi-zu'-rah nu'-me-ro do'-di-chi.

This is too small (large).
Questo è troppo piccolo (grande).
kwe'-sto è tròp-po pik'-ko-lo (grahn'-de).

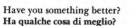

This is too tight (loose).
Questo è troppo stretto (largo).
kwe'-sto è tròp-po stret'-to (lahr'-go).

Do you have this in a lighter (darker) color?
Ha questo in colore più chiaro (oscuro)?
ah kwe'-sto in ko-lo'-re pyu kyah'-ro (o-sku'-ro)?

Have you something better?
Ha qualche cosa di meglio?
ah kwahl-ke kò-zah di mè-lyo?

What material is it made of?
Di che stoffa è?
di ke stòf-fah è?

How much is it?
Quanto costa?
kwahn'-to kò-stah?

That is too much.
E' troppo.
è tròp-po.

Can you let me have it for 200 lire?
Può darmelo per duecento lire.
pwò dahr'-me-lo per du-e-chèn-to li'-re?

I will let you have it for that pri
Vada per quel prezzo.
vah'-dah per kwel prè-tso.

That is fine. Please wrap it up.
Benissimo. Ne faccia un involto.
be-nis'-si-mo. ne fah'-chah un in-vol'-to.

I will take it with me.
Lo porterò con me.
lo por-te-rò kon me.

Please send it to my hotel.
Mi faccia la cortesia di mandarlo all'albergo.
mi fah'-chah lah kor-te-zi'-ah di mahn-dahr'-lo ahl ahl-bèr-go.

Please let me have a sales slip.
Per favore, mi dia una ricevuta.
per fah-vo'-re, mi di'-ah u'-nah ri-che-vu'-tah.

I would like to have this shipped to my home.
Vorrei che fosse spedito a domicilio.
vor-rè-y ke fos'-se spe-di'-to ah do-mi-chi'-lyo.

How much is this a meter?
A quanto al metro si vende questo?
ah kwahn'-to ahl mè-tro si ven'-de kwe'-sto?

What do you have for a five year old?
Che cos' ha per un bambino di cinque anni?
ke kò-zah' per un bahm-bi'-no di chin'-kwe ahn'-ni?

Do you have embroidered dresses?
Ha dei vestitini ricamati?
ah de'-y ve-sti-ti'-ni ri-kah-mah'-ti?

What is the price of that suede jacket?
Qual'è il prezzo di quella giacca di camoscio?
kwah-lè il prèt-tso di kwel'-lah jah'-kah di kah-mo'-sho?

Is this an imported fabric?
E' importata questa stoffa?
è im-por-tah'-tah kwe'-stah stof'-fah?

Let me see a silk dress.
Mi mostri un vestito di seta.
mi mò-stri un ves-ti'-to di se'-tah.

I like the black rayon one.
Mi piace quello di raion nero.
mi pyah'-che kwel'-lo di rah-yon' ne'-ro.

How long is the bright red one?
Quant'è lungo quello di rosso vivo?
kwahn'-tè lun'-go kwel'-lo di ro:'-so vi'-vo?

Do you have this shirt in blue?
Ha questa camicia in blu?
ah kwe'-stah kah-mi'-chah in blu?

Do you have my size in green?
Ha la mia misura in verde?
ah lah mi'-ah mi-zu'-rah in ver'-de?

Where is the leather goods counter?
Dove sono gli articoli di pelle?
do-vè so'-no lyi ahr-ti'-ko-li di pel'-le?

On the second floor.
Al secondo piano.
ahl se-kon'-do pyah'-no.

What is the price of that alligator handbag?
Quanto costa quella borsetta di coccodrillo?
kwahn'-to kò-stah kwel'-lah bor-set'-tah di kok-ko-dril'-lo.

I will take this belt.
Prenderò questa cinta.
pren-de-rò kwe'-stah chin'-tah.

I want to buy a pair of shoes.
Desidero comprare un paio di scarpe.
de-zi'-de-ro kom-prah'-re un pah'-yo di skahr'-pe.

Which color do you like: black, brown, or white?
Che colore le piace: nero, marrone o bianco?
ke ko-lo'-re le pyah'-che ne'-ro, mahr-ro'-ne o byahn'-ko?

I would like to see some brown shoes.
Vorrei vedere delle scarpe marroni.
vor-rè-y ve-de'-re del'- le skahr'-pe mahr-ro'-ni.

I am afraid these would not fit you; they are too narrow and
   also too short.
Temo che queste non le calzino bene; sono troppo strette e corte.
*te'-mo ke kwe'-ste non le kahl'-tsi-no bè-ne; so'-no tròp-po
   stret'-te e kor'-te.*

You are right. I need a larger size.
Ha ragione; mi occorre una misura più grande.
ah rah-jo'-ne; mi ok-kor'-re u'-nah mi-zu'-rah pyu grahn'-de.

What is the price of this perfume?
Quanto costa questo profumo?
kwahn'-to kò-stah kwe'-sto pro-fu'-mo?

Do you have a smaller (larger) bottle?
Ha una boccetta più piccola (grande)?
ah u'-nah bo-chet'-tah pyu pik'-ko-lah (grahn'-de)?

What is the price of these earrings?
Quanto costano questi orecchini?
kwahn'-to kò-stah-no kwe'-sti o-rek-ki'-ni?

Let me see that bracelet, please.
Per favore, mi faccia esaminare quel braccialetto.
per fah-vo'-re, mi fah'-chah e-zah-mi-nah'-re kwel brah-chah-let'-to.

I don't like this design.
Non mi piace questo disegno.
non mi pyah'-che kwe'-sto di-se'-nyo.

Is this tray sterling-silver?
E' d'argento puro questo vassoio?
è dahr-jen'-to pu'-ro kwe'-sto vahs-so'-yo?

Show me a silver tray.
Mi mostri un vassoio d'argento.
mi mo'-stri un vahs-so'-yo dahr-jèn-to.

You make silver articles to order, don't you?
Eseguiscóno articoli d'argento a commissione?
e-ze-gwis'-ko-no ahr-ti'-ko-li dahr-jèn-to ah kom-mis-syo'-ne?

LAUNDRY AND CLEANING

Please have this dry cleaned.
Per favore, mi faccia pulire questo a secco.
per fah-vo'-re, mi fah'-chah pu-li'-re kwe'-sto ah sek'-ko.

How long will it take?
Quanto tempo ci vorrà?
kwahn'to tèm-po chi vor-rah'?

I would like this suit pressed.
Vorrei far stirare quest'abito.
vor-rè-y fahr sti-rah'-ke kwe-stah'-bi-to.

Can I get it back this afternoon?
Lo posso avere di ritorno nel pomeriggio?
lo pòs-so ah-ve'-re di ri-tor'-no nel po-me-rij'-jo?

These shirts need laundering.
Queste camice sono da lavare.
kwe'-ste kah-mi'-che so'-no dah lah-vah'-re.

Please do not starch them.
Per piacere, le voglio senz'amido.
per pyah-che'-re, le vò-lyo sen-tsah'-mi-do.

Will you have them ready the day after tomorrow?
Saranno pronte per dopodomani?
sah-rahn'-no pron'-te per do-po-do-mah'-ni?

Please wash this dress.
Per favore, faccia lavare questo vestito.
per fah-vo'-re, fah'-chah lah-vah'-re kwe'-sto ve-sti'-to.

Please press the trousers.
Per favore, mi faccia stirare i calzoni.
per fah-vo'-re, mi fah'-chah sti-rah'-re i kahl-tso'-ni.

When can you have it ready?
Per quando sarà pronto?
per kwahn'-do sah-rah' pron'-to?

I must have it tomorrow.
Mi occorre domani.
mi ok-kor'-re do-mah'-ni.

Can you sew a button on my shirt?
Può attaccarmi un bottone alla camicia?
pwò aht-tahk-kahr'-mi un bot-to'-ne ah'lah kah-mi'-chah?

This is torn. Can you mend it?
Questo è strappato. Può rammendarlo?
kwe-sto è strahp-pah'-to. pwò rahm-men-dahr'-lo?

HAIRDRESSERS AND BARBERS

Could you direct me to a good hairdresser?
Può raccomandarmi un buon parrucchiere?
pwò rahk-ko-mahn-dahr'-mi un bwòn pahr-ruk-kyè-re?

I would like to have my hair washed and set.
Vorrei farmi lavare e mettere in piega i capelli.
vor-rè-y fahr'-mi lah-vah'-re e met'-te-re in pye'-gah i kah-pel'-li.

Would you like a permanent wave?
Vorrebbe una permanente?
vor-rèb-be u'nah per-mah-nen'-te?

What is the charge?
Quanto si paga?
kwahn'-to si pah'-gah?

I would like a haircut, please.
Mi tagli i capelli, per favore.
mi tah'-lyi i kah-pel'-li, per fah-vo'-re.

I want a trim.
Mi aggiusti i capelli, per favore.
mi ahj-ju'-sti i kah-pel'-li, per fah-vo'-re.

Not too much off the top.
Non ne tagli troppo di sopra.
non ne tah'-lyi tròp-po di so'-prah.

Cut it shorter, please.
Li tagli un pò più corti, per favore.
li tah'-lyi un pò pyu cor'-ti, per fah-vo'-re.

I want to have a shave.
Mi faccia la barba, per piacere.
mi fah'-chah la bahr-bah, per pyah-che'-re.

I would like to make an appointment for a manicure.
Vorrei un appuntamento per farmi fare le unghie.
vor-rè-y un ahp-pun-tah-men'-to per fahr'-mi fah'-re le un'-gye.

What time can you take me for a shampoo?
A che ora può farmi uno shampoo?
a ke o'-rah pwò fahr'-mi u'-no shahm-pu'?

GOING TO CHURCH

I would like to go to church.
Vorrei andare a chiesa.
vor-rè-y ahn-dah'-re ah kyè-zah?

Where is the (nearest) church?
Dov'è la chiesa (più vicina)?
do-vè lah kyè-zah (pyu vi-chi'-nah)?

Where is the cathedral?
Dov'è la cattedrale?
do-vè lah kaht-te-drah'-le?

Where is the synagogue?
Dov'è la sinagoga?
do-vè lah si-nah-gò-gah?

What kind of a church is this?
Di che fede è questa chiesa?
di ke fe'-de è kwe'-stah kyè-zah?

A Catholic church.
E' una chiesa cattolica.
è u'-nah kyè-zah kaht-tò-li-kah.

A Protestant church.
E' una chiesa protestante.
è u'-nah kyè-zah pro-te-stahn'-te.

At what time does the mass start?
A che ora comincia la messa?
ah ke o'-rah ko-min'-chah lah mes'-sah?

What church holds service in English?
In che chiesa si celebra in inglese?
in ke kyè-zah si che'-le-brah in in-gle'-ze?

May we attend this service?
Possiamo assistere a questa funzione?
pos-sya'-mo ahs-si'-ste-re ah kwe'-stah fun-tsyo'-ne?

I would like to see a priest (minister, rabbi).
Vorrei parlare con un prete (ministro, rabbino).
vor-rè-y pahr-lah-re kon un prè-te (mi-ni'-stro, rahb-bi'-no).

THEATER GOING

I should like two tickets for Tosca.   Who sings?
Vorrei due posti per La Tosca.   **Chi canta?**
vor-rè-y du'-e po'-sti per lah to'-skah.   *ki kahn'-tah?*

Have you any seats for tonight?
Ci sono dei posti disponibili per stasera?
chi so'-no de'-y po'-sti dis-po-ni-bi'-li per stah'-se-rah?

Can you show me a seating plan of La Scala di Milano?
Può mostrarmi una pianta della Scala di Milano?
pwò mo-strahr'-mi u'-nah pyahn'-tah del'-lah skah'-lah di mi-lah'-no?

Please let me have 2 orchestra (mezzanine, box, balcony) seats.
Per favore mi dia due biglietti di platea (prima galleria,
              palco, seconda galleria).
per fah-vo'-re, mi di'-ah du'-e bil-lyet'-ti di plah'-tè-ah
              (pahl'-ko; gahl-le-ri'-ah).

At what time does the performance start?
A che ora comincia la rappresentazione (lo spettacolo)?
ah ke o'-rah ko-min'-chah lah rahp-pre-zen-tah-tyso'-ne
              (lo spet-tah'-ko-lo)?

NIGHT LIFE

I want to visit several night clubs.
Vorrei visitare dei locali notturni.
vor-rè-y vi-zi-tah'-re de'-y lo-kah'-li not-tur'-ni.

I am interested in seeing a floor show.
Vorrei vedere qualche spettacolo.
vor-rè-y ve-de'-re kwahl'ke spet-tah'-ko-lo.

What places do you recommend?
Che locali può raccomandare?
ke lo-kah'-li pwò rahk-ko-mahn-dah'-re?

Are they very expensive?
Si spende molto?
si spèn-de mol'-to?

Is there a cover charge?
Si paga il coperto?
si pah'-gah il ko-pèr-to?

Are there any other charges?
C'è da pagare altro?
chè dah pah-gah'-re ahl'-tro?

What time does the floor show start?
A che ora comincia lo spettacolo?
ah ke o'-rah ko-min'-chah lo spet-tah'-ko-lo?

EXCHANGING MONEY

What is today's free market rate on the dollar?
Qual'è il cambio d'oggi del dollaro sul mercato libero?
kwahl-è il kahm'-byo dòj-ji del dol'-lah-ro sul mer-kah'-to li'-be-ro?

We do not pay anything but the legal rate.
Si cambia soltanto alla tariffa ufficiale.
si kahm'-byah sol-tahn'-to ahl'-lah tah-rif'-fah uf-fi-chah'-le.

I would like to cash a travelers check.
Vorrei cambiare un assegno di viaggio.
vor-rè-y kahm-byah'-re un ah-se'-nyo di vyah'-jo.

What is the rate of exchange?
A quant'è il cambio?
ah kwahn'-tè il kahm'-byo?

May I have 1,000 lire in small change?
Può darmi mille lire di spiccioli?
pwò dahr'-me mil'-le li'-re di spi'-cho-li?

Where can I buy a bank draft?
Dove posso procurare un vaglia bancario?
do'-ve pòs-so pro-ku-rah'-re un vah'-lyah bahn-kah'-ryo?

At the next window.
Allo sportello accanto.
ahl'-lo spor-tel'-lo ahk kahn'-to.

I would like to send a draft for 20,000 lire.
Vorrei mandare un vaglia di ventimila lire.
vor-rè-y mahn-dah'-re un vah'-lyah di ven-ti-mi'-lah li'-re.

COMMUNICATIONS

Post-Office

Where is the (nearest) post office?
Dov' è l'ufficio postale (più vicino)?
do-vè luf-fi'-cho po-stah'-le (pyu vi-chi'-no?)

Until what time is it open?
Fino a che ora è aperto?
fi'-no ah ke o'-rah è ah-per'-to?

It closes at five o'clock.
Chiude alle cinque.
kyu'-de ahl'-le chin'-kwe.

I want to send this special delivery.
Desidero mandare questa per espresso.
de-zi'-de-ro mahn-dah'-re kwe'-stah per e-sprès-so.

How much postage do I need for this letter?
Quanti francobolli ci vogliono per questa lettera?
kwahn'-ti frahn-ko-bol'-li chi vò-lyo-no per kwe'-stah lèt-te-rah?

I would like to have this letter registered.
Vorrei raccomandare questa lettera.
vor-rè-y rahk-ko-mahn-dah'-re kwe'-stah lèt-te-rah.

May I insure this parcel?
Posso assicurare questo pacco?
pòs-so ahs-si-ku-rah'-re kwe'-sto pahk'-ko?

What does it contain?   Books and printed matter.
Che cosa contiene?   **Libri e stampati.**
ke-kò-zah kon-tyè-ne?   *li'-bri e stahm-pah'-ti.*

Hold my mail until I call for it.
Trattenga la posta finchè vengo a ritirarla.
traht-tèn-gah lah po'-stah fin-kè vèn-go ah ri-ti-rahr'-lah.

Please forward my mail to Venice.
La prego d'inoltrare la mia corrispondenza a Venezia.
lah prè-go di-nol-trah'-re lah mi'-ah kor-ris-pon-dèn-tsah ah ve-nè-tsi-ah.

Telegrams and Cables

I would like to send a telegram to Paris.
Vorrei inviare un telegramma a Parigi.
vor-rè-y in-vyah'-re un te-le-grahm'-mah ah pah-ri'-dzi.

Please give me a blank for a foreign telegram.
Per favore, mi dia un modulo per l'estero.
per fah-vo'-re, mi di'-ah un mò-du lo per lè-ste-ro.

How much do fifteen words cost?
Quanto costano quindici parole?
kwahn'-to kò-stah-no kwin'-di-chi pah-rò-le?

Are you sending it day rate or night rate?
Lo vuol mandare a tariffa di giorno o di notte?
lo vwòl mahn-dah-re ah tah-rif'-fah di jor'-no o di nòt-te?

Send it immediately.
Lo mandi subito (immediatamente).
lo mahn'-di su'-bi-to (im-me-dyah-tah-mèn-te).

Telephoning

Where is the telephone (the telephone book)?
Dov'è il telefono (l'elenco telefonico)?
do-vè il te-lè-fo-no (le-lèn-ko te-le-fò-ni-ko)?

Operator, I have dialed the wrong number.
Signorina, mi sono sbagliato nel formare il numero.
si-nyo-ri'-nah, mi so'-no zbah-lyah-to nel for-mah'-re il nu'-me-ro.

This is Mr. Brown calling.
E' il Signor Brown che chiama.
è il si-nyor' Brown ke kyah'-mah.

Is Mr. Levi in?
E' in casa il Signor Levi?
è in kah'-zah il si-nyor' le'-vi?

No, he is not in.
No, non è in casa.
no, non è in kah'-zah.

When do you expect him?
Sa quando rientrerà?
sah kwahn'-do ri-en-tre-rah'?

May I speak to Mr. Rossi?
Vorrei parlare col Signor Rossi.
vor-rè-y pahr-lah'-re kol si-nyor' ros'-si?

Hold the wire, please, I'll put him on.
Aspetti un momento che lo chiamo.
ah-spèt-ti un mo-men'-to ke lo kyah'-mo.

I want to make a long distance call.
Vorrei l'interurbana.
vor-rè-y lin-ter-ur-bah'-nah.

I would like to call Chicago at 3:00.
Vorrei la comunicazione con Chicago alle tre.
vor-rè-y lah ko-mu-ni-kah-tsyo'-ne kon chi-kah'-go ahl'-le tre.

How much is a call to New York?
Quanto costa chiamare Nuova York?
kwahn'-to kò-stah kyah-mah'-re nwo'-vah york?

I am sorry, all the lines are busy.
Mi dispiace, tutte le linee sono occupate.
mi dis-pyah'-che, tut'-te le li'-ne-e so'-no ok-ku-pah'-te.

Signal me when the three minutes are over.
Mi avverta ai tre minuti.
mi ahv-ver'-tah ah-y tre mi-nu'-ti.

TOURIST INFORMATION

Where is the nearest tourist office?
Dov'è l'agenzia di turismo più vicina?
do-vè lah-jen-tsi'-ah di tu-ri'-zmo pyu vi-chi'-nah?

When is the next bus for Fiesole?
Quando parte il prossimo autobus per Fiesole?
kwahn'-do pahr'-te il pròs-si-mo ahu'-to-bus per fi-è-zo-le?

I wish to visit a place where there are no tourists.
Vorrei visitare un luogo dove non ci siano turisti.
vor-rè-y vi-si-tah'-re un lwò-go do'-ve non chi si'-ah-no tu-ris'-ti.

Is this town off the beaten track?
E' fuori di mano questa cittadina?
è fwò-ri di mah'-no kwe'-stah chit-tah-di'-nah?

Yes, very much so.
Sì, di parecchio.
si, di pah-rek'-kyo.

Is it difficult to reach?
E' difficile arrivarci?
è dif-fi'-chi-le ahr-ri-vahr'-chi?

No, there is frequent bus service.
No, c'è servizio regolare d'autobus.
no, chè ser-vi'-tsyo re-go-lah'-re dah-u'-to-bus.

Does it have a good, inexpensive hotel?
Vi è là un buon albergo che non sia caro?
vi è lah un bwòn ahl-bèr-go ke non si'-ah kah'-ro?

YOUR HEALTH ABROAD

I have an upset stomach.
Ho lo stomaco indisposto.
ò lo sto'-mah-ko in-dis-po'-sto.

I don't feel well.
Non mi sento bene.
non mi sèn-to bè-ne.

I need a doctor (dentist, oculist) who speaks English.
Ho bisogno d'un medico (dentista, oculista) che parli inglese.
ò bi-zo'-nyo dun mè-di-ko (den-ti'-stah, o-ku-li-stah) ke pahr'-li in-gle'-ze?

I cut myself.
Mi sono tagliato.
mi so'-no tah-lyah'-to.

I have sprained (broken) my ankle.
Ho storto (fratturato) la caviglia.
ò stòr-to (fraht-tu-rah'-to) lah kah-vi'-lyah.

I have a fever.
Ho la febbre.
ò lah feb'-bre.

I have a bad cold.
Ho un brutto raffreddore.
ò un brut'-to rahf-fred-do'-re.

Will I have to stay in bed?
Dovrò restare a letto?
do-vrò re-stah'-re ah lèt-to?

Where does it hurt?
Dove le fa male?
do've le fah mah'-le?

My back (foot, arm, leg, throat, head) hurts.
Mi duole la schiena (il piede, il braccio, la gamba, la gola, la testa).
mi dwò-le lah skye'-nah (il pyè-de, il brahch'-cho, lah gahm'-bah, lah go'-lah, lah tè-stah).

I have a toothache.
Mi fa male un dente.
mi fah mah'-le un den-te.

Must the tooth be filled?
Dovrà essere piombato il dente?
do-vrah' ès-se-re pyom-bah'-to il dèn-te?

What is your fee, doctor?
Quant'è l'onorario, dottore?
kwahn-tè lo-no-rah'-ryo, dot-to'-re?

Where is the nearest drugstore?
Dov'è la farmacia più vicina?
do-vè lah fahr-mah-chi'-ah pyu vi-chi'-nah?

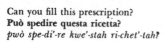

Can you fill this prescription?
Può spedire questa ricetta?
pwò spe-di'-re kwe'-stah ri-chet'-tah?

When will it be ready?
Quando sarà pronta?
kwahn'-do sah-rah' pron'-tah?

I have broken my glasses.
Mi si sono rotti gli occhiali.
mi si so'-no rot'-ti lyi ok-kyah'-li.

Can you put in a new lens?
Può inserire delle nuove lenti?
pwò in-se-ri'-re del'-le nwò-ve lèn-ti?

SPORTS AND AMUSEMENTS

Fishing and Hunting

I need a rod and reel, some line, and hooks.
Mi bisognano una canna da pesca con bobina, una lenza e degli ami.
*mi bi-zo'-nyah-no u'-nah kahn'-nah dah pes'-kah.kon bo-bi'-nah,
u'-nah lèn-zah e de'-lyi ah'-mi.*

Where can we rent a boat?
Dove si può noleggiare una barca?
do've si pwò no-lej-jah'-re u'-nah bahr'-kah?

I need a gun for hunting.
Mi occorre un fucile da caccia.
mi o-kòr-re un fu-chi'-le dah kah'-chah.

Where can I buy ammunition?
Dove posso comprare le pallottole?
do'-ve pòs'-so kom-prah'-re le pahl-lot'-to-le?

What is the best place for hunting?
Qual'è il miglior posto per andare a caccia?
kwahl è il mi-lyor' po'-sto per ahn-dah'-re ah kah'-chah?

The hunting season is from December to March.
La stagione di caccia è da dicembre a marzo.
la stah-jo'-ne di kah'-chah è dah di-chèm-bre ah mahr'-tso.

Swimming and Bathing

Can I rent a suit?
Si può prendere in affitto un costume da bagno?
Si pwò pren'-de-re in ahf-fit'-to un kos-tu'-me dah bah'-nyo?

Is the pool chlorinated?
E' clorinata la piscina?
è klo-ri-nah'-tah lah pi-shi'-nah?

I would like to rent a towel.
Vorrei un ascugamano in affitto.
vor-rè-y un ah-shu-gah-mah'-no in ahf-fit'-to.

What is the charge?
Quanto si paga?
kwahn'-to si pah'-gah?

Is the towel included in the price of admission?
E' incluso l'asciugamano nel biglietto d'entrata?
è in-klu'-zo lah-shu-gah-mah'-no nel bi-lyet'-to den-trah'-tah?

Do you sell suntan oil?
Si vende olio per abbronzare?
si ven'-de ò-lyo per ahb-bron-zah'-re?

I would like to rent a cabin.
Vorrei affittare una cabina (camerino).
vor-rè-y ahf-fit-tah'-re u'-nah kah-bi'-nah (kah-me-ri'-no).

On the Golf Course

I would like to rent a set of golf clubs, please.
Vorrei prendere in affitto un assortimento di bastoni.
vor-rè-y pren'-de-re in ahf-fit'-to un ahs-sor-ti-men'-to di bah-sto'-ni.

Will you want to hire a caddy?
Vuol impegnare un caddi?
vwòl impe-nyah'-re un kahd'-di?

Will you provide me with a good caddy?
Mi vuol assegnare un buon caddi?
mi vwòl ahs-se-nyah'-re un bwòn kahd'-di?

I wish to buy some golf balls.
Vorrei comprare delle palle da golf.
vor-rè-y kom-prah'-re del'-le pahl'-le dah golf.

Where do I tee off?
Dov' è la piazzuola di partenza?
do-vè lah pyahts-tswo'-lah di pahr-ten'-tsah?

Caddy, give me the driver.
Caddi (ragazzino), mi dia il driver.
kahd'-di (rah-gah-tsi'-no) mi dì'-ah il driver.

At the Tennis Courts

What is the charge for the use of the courts?
Quanto si paga per l'uso d'un campo di gioco?
kwahn'-to si pah'-gah per lu'-zo dun kahm'-po di jò-ko?

Can I have a racket?
Posso procurarmi una racchetta?
pòs-so pro-ku-rahr'-mi u'-nah rahk-ket'-tah?

I would like to buy a can of balls.
Vorrei comprare un barattolo di palle da tennis.
vor-rè-y kom-prah'-re un bah-raht'-to-lo di pahl'-le dah ten'-nis.

Where is the men's locker room?
Dov'è lo spogliatoio per uomini?
do-vè lo spo-lyah-to'-yo per uo'-mi-ni?

Baseball

Two seats, please.
Due posti, per favore.
du-e po'-sti, per fah-vo'-re.

Which team is leading the league?
Quale squadra primeggia nella lega?
kwah'-le skwah'-drah pri-mej'-jah nel'-lah le'-gah?

Can you tell me the score?
Può dirmi qual'è il punteggio?
pwò dir'-mi kwahl è il pun-tej'-jo?

Carnival

Will you take part in the parade?
Vuol partecipare alla sfilata (al concorso)?
vwòl pahr-te-chi-pah'-re ahl'-lah sfi-lah'-tah (ahl kon-kor'-so)?

How can we? We have no costumes.
Come possiamo? Non abbiamo costume (abito da festa).
kò-me pos-syah'-mo? non ahb-byah'-mo ko-stu'-me (ah'-bi-to dah fè-stah).

Why not get seats in the stands?
Perchè non ci sediamo sul palco?
per-kè non chi se-dyah'-mo sul pahl'-ko?

Other Sports

May I have 2 tickets, close to the ringside?
Può darmi due posti accanto al ring?
pwò dahr'-mi du'-e po'-sti ahk-kahn'-to ahl ring?

How much will they cost? Is it a championship fight?
Quanto costano? **È un incontro di campionato?**
kwahn'-to ko'-stah-no? *è un in-kon'-tro di kahm-pyo-nah'-to?*

How long have the contestants been racing?
Da quanto tempo gareggiano i contendenti?
dah kwahn'-to tèm-po gah-rej'-jah-no i kon-ten-dèn-ti?

How many kms. do they cover?
Quanti kilometri devono fare?
kwahn'-ti ki-lo'-me-tri dè-vo-no fah'-re?

How many racers are taking part?
Quanti corridori partecipano?
kwahn'-ti kor-ri-do'-ri pahr-te'-chi-pah-no?

What is the price range for tickets?
A che prezzi si vendono i biglietti?
ah kè prè-tsi si ven'-do-no i bi-lyet'-ti?

Can I rent skis?
Posso avere in affitto un paio di sci?
pos'-so ah-ve'-re in ahf-fit'-to un pah'-yo di shi?

CONDUCTING BUSINESS

I wish to apply for a visa.
Vorrei far istanza per un visto.
vor-rè-y fahr is-tahn'-tzah per un vi'-sto.

When will my visa be ready?
Quando sarà pronto il visto?
kwahn'-do sah-rah' pron'-to il vi'-sto?

Here is my identity card.
Ecco la mia carta d'identità.
èk-ko lah mi'-ah kahr'-tah di-den-ti-tah'.

For how long a period is my card valid?
Per quanto tempo è válida la mia carta?
per kwahn'-to tèm-po è vah'-li-dah lah mi'-ah kahr'-tah?

If I move from here, what must I do?
Se mi trasferisco di qui, cosa devo fare?
se mi trah-sfe-ri'-sko di kwi, kò-zah dè-vo fah'-re?

I have never been bankrupt.
Non sono mai stato in bancarotta.
non so'-no mah'-y stah'-to in bahn-kah-rot'-tah.

I would like to contact a firm that makes furniture.
Vorrei stabilire relazioni con una ditta che produca mobili.
vor-rè-y stah-bi-li'-re re-lah-tsyo'-ni kon u'nah dit'-tah
        ke pro-du'-kah mò-bi-li.

Whom would you recommend?
Chi raccomanderebbe?
ki rahk-ko mahn-de-rèb-be?

I represent an American firm.
Rappresento una ditta americana.
rahp-pre-zèn-to u'-nah dit'-tah ah-me-ri-kah'-nah.

I am a traveling salesman.
Sono un commesso viaggiatore.
so'-no un kom-mes'-so vyahj-jah-to'-re.

May I show you these samples?
Permette che le mostri questi campioni?
per-met'-te ke le mo'-stri kwe'-sti kahm-pyo'-ni?

I am here to survey the market.
Sono qui per studiare il mercato.
so'-no kwi per stu dyah'-re il mer-kah'-to.

I need a local distributor for my product.
Ho bisogno di un rappresentante distributore del mio prodotto.
ò bi-zo'-nyo di un rahp-pre-zen-tahn'-te di-stri-bu-to'-re
        del mi'-o pro-dot'-to.

Where can I check on the firm's credit rating?
Dove posso avere un rapporto finanziario sulla ditta?
do'-ve pòs-so ah-ve'-re un rahp-pòr-to fi-nahn-tsyah'-ryo sul'-lah dit'-tah?

Why We Make This Generous Offer

There are three important reasons why the Institute for Language Study is pleased to make this special Free Recording and Sample Lesson offer:

First, never before have there been so many fascinating opportunities open to those who speak foreign languages fluently. Besides the cultural and travel benefits, there are many practical dollars-and-cents advantages—and an ever-increasing number of interesting, well-paying jobs.

The Natural Method

Second, our long experience in the language field has convinced us that the "learn-by-listening" method is the fastest, most convenient and most effective one. It enables you to learn *naturally*—the way you learned English as a child. You acquire a perfect accent and perfect grammar—because that's all you hear.

Just Listen—and Learn

Finally, our professional standing in the field of languages has enabled us to make these generous arrangements with one of the foremost language schools—the inventors of the "learn-by-listening" method. And we are pleased to provide this service for those of our students who want to speak and understand a foreign language "like a native."

There is no obligation and *no salesman will call.* Just mail the card TODAY for your FREE Recording.

What Others Say:

Bob Hope says... "I am studying the course in French ... I think it's a great way to study a language."

Enjoyed by Children "It is surprising how much our two children have absorbed by listening."
—Mrs. C.M.J.

"A Good Investment" "Just returned from Mexico ... Course good investment!"
—Phillips B. Iden

Institute for Language Study
19 Newtown Turnpike, Westport, CT 06880

Can this product be manufactured here?
Si può fabbricare questo prodotto localmente?
si pwò fahb-bri-kah'-re kwe'-sto pro-dot'-to lo-kahl-mèn-te?

How large is your factory?
Quant' è grande la sua fabbrica?
kwahn'-tè grahn'-de lah su'-ah fahb'bri-kah?

How many people do you employ?
Quanto personale impiega?
kwahn'-to per-so-nah'-le im-pye'-gah?

What is your capital?
Quant' è il capitale investito?
kwahn-tè il kah-pi-tah'-le in-ve-sti'-to?

May I inspect your plant?
Permette che si faccia un giro d'ispezione della fabbrica?
per-met'-te ke si fah'-chah un ji'-ro di-spe-tsyo'-ne del'-lah fahb'-bri-kah?

I would like bank references.
Vorrei delle referenze bancarie.
vor-rè-y del'-le re-fe-rèn-tse bahn-kah'-rye.

I am authorized to pay for goods in dollars.
Sono autorizzato a pagare per la merce in dollari.
so'-no ah-u-to-ri-dzah'-to ah pah-gah'-re per lah mer'-che in dòl-lah-ri.

Where can you ship the merchandise?
Dove può spedire la merce?
do'-ve pwò spe-di'-re lah mèr-che?

OUTLINE OF ITALIAN GRAMMAR

Although, for purposes of everyday practical needs, you will be able to get by with some stock of common Italian words and phrases, it is advisable also to have some understanding of the parts of speech and their various forms as well as of the manner in which Italian sentences are constructed. In the following pages we have attempted to present the "highlights" of Italian grammar very concisely, so as to enable you to understand the how and why of the phrases in this book. This survey is of necessity brief, but the main facts for your daily needs have been covered.

THE ARTICLE

1.1. The forms of the definite article in Italian are:

	Singular	Plural
Masculine	**il; lo[1]; l'[2]** (the)	**i; gli[1]; gl'[3]** (the)
Feminine	**la; l'[2]** (the)	**le** (the)

Examples: *il capitano* (the captain); *lo stile* (the style), *lo zio* (the uncle); *l'amico* (the friend); *i capitani* (the captains); *gli stili* (the styles), *gli zii* (the uncles); *gl' Italiani* (the Italians); *la motonave* (the motor ship); *l'anima* (the soul); *le motonavi* (the motor ships), *le anime* (the souls).

1.2. The definite articles are contracted with a number of prepositions:

		il	lo	la	l'	i	gli	le
a	(to, at)	al	allo	alla	all'	ai	agli	alle
da	(from)	dal	dallo	dalla	dall'	dai	dagli	dalle
di	(of)	del	dello	della	dell'	dei	degli	delle
in	(in)	nel	nello	nella	nell'	nei	negli	nelle
su	(on)	sul	sullo	sulla	sull'	sui	sugli	sulle

[1] *Lo* is used before nouns begining with *z* or *s* followed by a consonant in the singular; *gli* is used in the plural.

[2] *L'* is used before nouns beginning with a vowel.

[3] *Gl'* is used before nouns beginning with *i*.

Con contracts only with *il* and *i* to *col* and *coi* in modern Italian.

1.3. The definite article in Italian is used more often than in English.

1.4. The forms of the indefinite article in Italian are:

	Singular	*Plural*[3]
Masculine	un; uno[1] (a, an)	dei; degli[4] (some)
Feminine	una; un'[2] (a, an)	delle (some)

Examples: *un orologio* (a watch), *un fiore* (a flower); *uno scherzo* (a joke, trick), *uno zucchino* (a squash); *una formica* (an ant); *un'amica* (a girl friend); *dei fiori* (some flowers); *degli zeri* (some zeros); *degli uomini* (some men); *degl' Italiani* (some Italians); *delle strade* (some streets); *delle formiche* (some ants); *delle amiche* (some girl friends).

1.5. The indefinite article is not used so often in Italian as in English.

1.6. Both the definite and indefinite articles agree in gender and number with the noun they modify.

1.7. The partitive article, which is placed before names of things in order to indicate part of the whole, consists of the preposition *di* with one of the different forms of the definite article (see 1.2): *Ho dei fiori* (I have flowers); *Desidero della carne* (I want some meat). The partitive article generally is not used in negative and interrogative sentences: *Non abbiamo carne* (We have no meat); *Ha danaro?* (Have you [any] money?).

THE NOUN

2.1. All nouns in Italian are either masculine or feminine. Almost all nouns ending in -*o* are masculine and most of those ending in -*a* are feminine. Nouns ending in -*e* are either masculine or feminine. Nearly all of the few nouns which end in -*i* are feminine.

---

[1] *Uno* is used before nouns beginning with z or s followed by a consonant.

[2] *Un'* is used before nouns beginning with a vowel.

[3] There is no plural of the indefinite article, but the definite article in combination with the preposition *di* acquires the meaning of "some" and functions as the plural of the indefinite article.

[4] *Degli* is used before nouns beginning with z, before nouns beginning with s followed by a consonant, and before nouns beginning with a vowel.

2.2. There is a number of nouns of frequent occurrence that change meaning according to gender:

il gambo (stalk, stem)	*la gamba* (leg)
il foglio (sheet [of paper])	*la foglia* (leaf)
il costo (price, cost)	*la costa* (the coast)
il fine (purpose)	*la fine* (end, close)
il pianto (the crying)	*la pianta* (the plant)
il colpo (the blow)	*la colpa* (the fault)
il collo (neck)	*la colla* (glue)
lo scalo (landing place)	*la scala* (stairs, ladder)
il modo (manner, means)	*la moda* (style, fashion)
il punto (point [of time or place])	*la punta* (the extremity)

2.3. The masculine nouns, regardless of how they end in the singular, form their plural by changing the singular ending to -*i*. Feminine nouns ending in -*a* change to -*e* in the plural, and those ending in -*e* to -*i*. Nouns ending in -*i* or -*u* have the same form for singular and plural.

2.4. Italian speakers use a number of diminutives formed by the suffixes *ino*, -*ello*, -*etto*, -*uccio*, -*olino*, -*icino* denoting smallness, sometimes coupled with grace, like *Paolo* (Paul), *Paolino;* and a number of augmentatives formed by the suffixes -*one*, -*accio* and -*otto* denoting bigness; sometimes, as in the case of -*accio*, in a disparaging sense.

THE ADJECTIVE

3.1. The adjective agrees in gender and number with the noun it modifies. The masculine plural form is used when the adjective modifies two or more nouns, one of which is masculine: *La camera e il servizio sono buoni.* (The room and the service are good).

3.2. There are two classes of adjectives in Italian:

a) Those which end in -*o* in the masculine singular and have four forms: *il ragazzo pigro* (the lazy boy), *i ragazzi pigri* (the lazy boys); *la ragazza pigra* (the lazy girl), *le ragazze pigre* (the lazy girls).

b) Those which end in -*e* in the singular and have only two forms, the masculine and the feminine forms being identical for each number: *il ragazzo intelligente* (the intelligent boy), *i ragazzi intelligenti; la ragazza intelligente* (the intelligent girl), *le ragazze intelligenti.*

3.3. In Italian the usual position of the descriptive adjectives is after the noun they modify: *La motonave bianca* (the white motorship). The demonstrative, indefinite, interrogative, and possessive adjectives, the numerals and the adjectives *molto* (much) and *tutto* (all) precede the noun they modify: *questo libro* (this book); *qualche cosa* (some thing or something); *quale lettera* (which letter); *mio zio* (my uncle); *tre bauli* (three trunks); *molti amici* (many friends); *tutta la gente* (all the people). Note that *tutto* used with a noun requires the article before the noun.

The following common adjectives usually precede the noun unless they are modified by an adverb: *bello* (beautiful), *buono* (good), *brutto* (ugly), *cattivo* (bad), *giovane* (young), *grande* (big), *ottimo* (excellent), *piccolo* (small), *povero* (poor).

Some adjectives change in meaning depending on whether they precede or follow the noun. The most common of them are: *grande, nuovo, vecchio: una grande città* (a great city) *una città grande* (a big city); *una nuova automobile* (a new [another or different] car), *una automobile nuova* (a new [brand-new] car); *un vecchio amico* (an old friend of long standing), *un amico vecchio* (a friend old in age).

3.4. The comparative is formed by placing *più* (more) before the adjective: *più bello* (more beautiful). The superlative is formed by adding the article to the comparative: *il più bello, la più bella* (the most beautiful). Some adjectives have an irregular comparison in addition to their regular one; the most common are:

buono (good)	*migliore* (better)	*il migliore* (best)
cattivo (bad)	*peggiore* (worse)	*il peggiore* (worst)
grande (big)	*maggiore* (larger)	*il maggiore* (largest)
piccolo (small)	*minore* (smaller)	*il minore* (smallest)

3.5. The **cardinal, ordinal** and **fractional numerals** are listed in the Counting section of the Conversational sentences. The cardinal numbers are invariable, except *uno (un, una)* (one) and *mille* (one thousand) which has *mila* as plural. *Cento* (one hundred) and *mille* do not take *un* before them.

3.6. The ordinal numbers agree in number and gender with the nouns: *il secondo giorno* (the second day); *la terza casa* (the third house). Beginning with *undici* (eleven), the ordinal numbers in Italian are formed by dropping the final vowel of the number and adding *-esimo: undici* (eleven) becomes *undicesimo*. However, numbers ending in *-tre* remain intact: *ventitre* (twenty-three) becomes *ventitreesimo*.

THE PRONOUN

4.1.a. The personal pronouns are:

English equivalent	Subject	Indirect object	Direct object	Disjunctive (used after prepositions)
I, to me, me, (with) me, etc.⎱	io	mi	mi	me
you (familiar, singular)⎱	tu	ti	ti	te
you (polite, singular)⎱	Lei	Le	La	Lei
he	egli	gli	lo	lui
she	ella	le	la	lei
it (masc.)	esso	gli	lo	esso
it (fem.)	essa	le	la	essa
we	noi	ci	ci	noi
you (familiar, plural)⎱	voi	vi	vi	voi
you (polite, plural)⎱	Loro	Loro	Li (m.) Le (f.)	Loro
they (persons)	essi (m.) esse (f.)	loro	li (m.) le (f.)	loro
they (objects)	essi (m.) esse (f.)	loro	li (m.) le (f.)	essi (m.) esse (f.)

4.1.b. The familiar forms are principally used in addressing close friends, relatives and children. *Voi*, the form for the familiar plural, is also used frequently as a singular form of address, but is less polite than *Lei*.

4.1.c. The normal position of the object pronouns is before the verb, with the exception of *loro: lo vedo* (I see him). In compound tenses they are placed before the auxiliary verb, and the past participle agrees with the direct object: *le ho viste* (I have seen them [fem.]). The direct object pronouns are attached to the word *ecco* and to infinitives: *eccola* (there she is); *voglio vederlo* (I want to see him or it). The object pronouns are attached to the *tu, noi* and *voi* forms of the affirmative imperative: *mandiamole il denaro* (let's send her the money); *dagli il libro* (give him the book). But: *parlate loro* (speak to them).

4.1.d. When a verb has both a direct and an indirect object pronoun, the pronouns *mi, ti, ci, vi* and *si* (see **4.2**) change the *i* into *e* before *lo, la, le, li* and *ne* (see **4.6.c**). Both *gli* and *le* are written *glie* in conjunction with direct object pronouns, with which they form one word. Examples: *te lo do* (I give it to you); *ce ne scrivono* (they write to us about it); *gliene parlo* (I speak to him or her about it); *gliela manderò* (I will send it [fem.] to him or her); *La prego di raccontarmelo* (I request you to tell it to me), *non glielo posso dire* or *non posso dirglielo* (I am unable to tell it to you).

4.1e. In compound tenses, the object pronouns generally precede the auxiliary verb, as in *Le è piaciuto il romanzo che Le ho prestato? Sì, l'ho letto e Glielo ho restuito per la posta.* (Did you like the novel I lent you? Yes, I read it and returned it to you by mail.) *Ce ne siamo andati* (we have gone away; from the idiom *andarsene*, to go away).

4.1.f. The pronouns can be accompanied by the word *stesso, -a, -i, -e (self)* for special emphasis: *io stesso ho telefonato* (I myself telephoned); *egli stesso* (or *ella stessa*) *Le ha scritto* (he himself [or she herself] has written to you).

4.2 Reflexive pronouns. The object pronouns of the first (*mi* for the singular and *ci* for the plural) and second (*ti* for the singular and *vi* for the plural) persons have a reflexive meaning when they refer to the same person as the subject. The reflexive pronoun for the second (polite form) and third persons of both singular and plural is *si*. The reflexive pronouns always precede the verb (also the auxiliary verb), except for the infinitive and the *tu, noi* and *voi* forms of the affirmative imperative. Examples: *io mi lavo le mani* (I wash my hands); *alzatevi!* (get up!); *Carlo vuole divertirsi* (Charles wants to enjoy himself). *Si* can also mean "each other" when expressing reciprocal action: *si scrivono* (they write to each other); *ci siamo veduti spesso* (we've often seen each other). Note that the compound tenses of verbs used reflexively are always formed with the auxiliary verb *essere* (and **never** with *avere*).

4.3.a. The possessive adjectives are:

Singular		Plural		
Masculine	Feminine	Masculine	Feminine	English
(il) mio	(la) mia	(i) miei	(le) mie	*my*
(il) tuo	(la) tua	(i) tuoi	(le) tue	*your (fam.)*
(il) suo	(la) sua	(i) suoi	(le) sue	*your (pol.), his, her*
(il) nostro	(la) nostra	(i) nostri	(le) nostre	*our*
(il) vostro	(la) vostra	(i) vostri	(le) vostre	*your*
(il) loro	(la) loro	(i) loro	(le) loro	*your, their*

The possessive adjectives agree in number and gender with the thing possessed and not with the possessor: *I miei bauli sono in cabina* (My trunks are in the cabin). They are generally preceded by the definite article except in the case of nouns denoting close relatives in the singular and not modified in any way: *il mio libro* (my book); *mia sorella* (my sister); *la mia cara zia* (my dear aunt).

4.3.b. The possessive pronouns have exactly the same form as the possessive adjectives. Note that after the verb *essere*, a pronoun denoting possession is used without an article: *E' suo? Sì, è mio.* (Is it yours? Yes, it is mine).

4.4.a. The interrogative adjectives are: *Che* (what); *quale, -i* (which); *quanto, -a, -i, -e* (how much, how many): *Che sigarette si vendono?* (What cigarettes are sold?) (*Che* is used for both the singular and the plural.) *Quale città preferisce?* (Which city do you prefer?) (*Quale* is both masculine and feminine; the plural for both is *quali*.) *Quanti biglietti desidera?* (How many tickets do you want?); *Quanto ha pagato?* (How much did you pay?).

4.4.b. The interrogative pronouns are: *Chi* (who, whom [for both genders both sing. and pl.]); *che cosa* or *che* or *cosa* (what); *quale, -i* (which, which ones); *di chi* (whose): *Chi è quella signora?* (Who is that lady?); *Con chi va?* (With whom are you going?); *Che (che cosa, cosa) desidera comprare?* (What do you want to buy?); *Qual' è il suo cappello?* (Which is your hat?); *Di chi è questo passaporto?* (Whose passport is this?).

4.5.a. The demonstrative adjectives are:

1. *Questo, -a, -i, -e* (this), indicating an object which is near the person who speaks: *In quest' albergo si mangia bene* (In this hotel one eats well).

2. *Codesto, -a, -i, -e* (that), indicating an object which is near the person addressed: *Questo libro mi piace più di codesto* (I like this book better than that. [literally: This book pleases me more than that]).

3. *Quel, quella, quello, quei, quelle, quegli* (that), indicating an object which is far from both the person speaking and the person addressed: *Quel giorno* (that day); *quella sera* (that evening); *quello specchio* (that mirror); *quei conti* (those bills); *quelle signore* (those ladies); *quegli sbagli* (those errors).

4. *Stesso* (same) and *medesimo* (same), indicating something of which one has previous knowledge. (Both take the definite article). (See 4.1.f).

4.5.b. There is no difference in form between **the demonstrative pronouns** *questo, quello,* and *codesto* and the corresponding demonstrative adjectives, except that *quello* as a pronoun has only four forms: *quello, -a, -i, -e.* Note that *codesto* is no longer used as a pronoun except in a deprecatory sense. Another demonstrative pronoun is *ciò* (this, that) which may be used as subject or as object of the verb referring to something which has already been said.

4.6.a. The most common **indefinite adjectives** are:

1. With four forms: *altro, -a, -i, -e* (other); *alcuno* (some); *certo* (certain); *molto* (much); *nessuno* (no . . .); *poco* (little); *troppo* (too much); *tutto* (every). Note that *tutto, -a, -i, -e* takes the article before the noun: *tutto il mese* (all month).

2. With one form always used in the singular: *ogni* (every); *qualche* (some); *qualunque* (any); and *qualsiasi* (any).

4.6.b. The most common **indefinite pronouns** are: *nessuno* (nobody, no one); *nulla* or *niente* (nothing); *ognuno* (anybody, any one, everyone, everybody); *qualcuno* (some one, somebody); *chiunque* (whoever, anybody who); *tutto, tutti* (all, everything); *alcuni* (some); *altri* (others).

Note that the negative words *nessuno, nulla, niente* when placed after the verb take *non* before the verb: *Nessuno mi parla* or *Non mi parla nessuno* (No one [or nobody] speaks to me); *Nulla vedo* or *Non vedo nulla* (I don't see anything). The construction with *non* is used more often.

4.6.c. In addition to its other uses as a personal pronoun (see 4.1.d) and adverb (see **6.4**), *ne* is also used as an indefinite pronoun: *Ne ha?* (Do you have any?) *Sì, ne ho* (Yes, I have some).

4.7. The **relative pronouns** are:

1. *Che* (who, whom, that, which) is the most common of the relative pronouns. It is used both as the subject or the direct object of a verb: *L'uomo che le ha portato questo è mio cugino* (The man who brought you this is my cousin). *Mi piace la pipa che mi ha data* (I like the pipe [which] you gave me). Note in the above sentence that the word "which" or "that" (*che*), which may be and is often omitted in English, may never be omitted in Italian.

2. *Cui* means *whom, which* when it is preceded by a preposition; and *whose* when it is preceded by the definite article or a contraction: *Le ragazze di cui parla Lei sono le mie sorelle* (The girls of whom you are talking are my sisters). *Ecco l'uomo il cui fratello è dottore* (Here is the man whose brother is a doctor).

3. *Il quale, la quale, i quali, le quali* (who, whom, which) are used instead of *che* and *cui* when there is a possibility of ambiguity.

4. *Ciò* is used when the word "what" means "that which": *Ciò che ella dice non è vero* (What she says is not true).

5. *Chi* (he who, him who, the one who); *colui che* (m.), *colei che* (f.) are used with a singular verb. *Coloro che* (they who, etc.) takes a plural verb.

THE PREPOSITION

5.1. Prepositional usage is largely idiomatic. You should form the habit of observing and learning, through repetition and practice, the prepositional usages which differ from English as you encounter them.

The most common prepositions in Italian are: *a* ([frequently *ad* before vowels] to; at, in; for, etc.); *da* (from; at; for; by, etc.); *di* (of; by); *in* (in, into); *per* (for; by means of); *su* (on; about; over, upon); *tra* (between, among). For their contractions with the definite article, see **1.2.**

5.2. The preposition *di* is used to indicate ownership *(Il passaporto di Giovanni* [John's passport]) or the material of which an object is made *(una veste di seta* [a silk dress]). (See also **1.7.**) Note: *una tazza di caffè* (a cup of coffee); *una tazza da caffè* (a coffee cup).

5.3. In Italian, nouns never function as adjectives by merely preceding the noun they modify. Their relation with the noun they modify is expressed by means of a preposition preceding the modifying noun: *hair tonic* (tonico per capelli); *hair net* (retina di capelli); *landlady* (padrona di casa).

5.4. There is an idiomatic use of prepositions in Italian in the case of certain verbs when they are followed by the infinitive, e.g., *Ha imparato a condurre.* (He has learned to drive); *Mi ha chiesto di venire* (He has asked me to come).

THE ADVERB

6.1. In Italian most of the adverbs of manner are formed by adding *-mente* to the singular feminine form of the adjective: *lento, -a* (slow), *lentamente* (slowly); *breve* (brief), *brevemente* (briefly).

Adjectives ending in *-ale, -ele, -ile, -ole, -are* and *-ore* drop the final *e* before adding *-mente*: *generale* (general), *generalmente* (generally).

Many adjectives in the masculine singular form may be used as adverbs, although the alternate adverbial form may also be used: *chiaro, chiaramente* (clearly).

6.2. The comparative of adverbs is formed by placing *più* before the adverb; and the superlative by placing *il più* before it. Four very common adverbs have irregular comparatives: *bene* (well), *meglio* (better); *male* (badly), *peggio* (worse); *molto* (much), *più* (more); *poco* (little), *meno* (less).

6.3. *Dove* is used to translate the word "where": *Dove si trova l'ufficio postale (la posta)?* (Where is the post office?); *Non è contento dove si trova* (He is not happy where he is). Other frequently used adverbs are: *allora* (then); *come* (as, like, how); *così* (so, thus); *invece* (instead); *almeno* (at least); *altrimenti* (otherwise); *anzi* (on the contrary); *forse* (perhaps); *abbastanza* (enough); *ancora* (yet, still); *solo, soltanto, solamente* (only); *tanto* (so much); *affatto* (quite, at all); *mai* (never); *neppure* (not even, nor); *prima* (first); *dopo* (afterwards).

6.4. There are three adverbs which have identical forms used as pronouns (See **4.1** and **4.2**): *ci* and *vi* may be used interchangeably for *here* and *there* when they refer in a non-emphatic way to a place already mentioned. *Ne* is used to express *thence, from there*: *Vado in Italia e ci resterò due mesi* (I'm going to Italy and will stay there two months); *E'un bel giardino. Vi* (or *Ci*) *sono molti fiori* (It's a fine garden. There are many flowers in it); *Quando sei venuto da Roma? Ne sono venuto ieri* (When did you come from Rome? I have come yesterday from there).

THE CONJUNCTION

7.1. Coordinating conjunctions join sentences, clauses, phrases and words of equal rank. The most common ones are, *e* (and), *o* (or), *ma* (but), *però* (however) and the correlatives *o . . . o* (either . . . or), *nè . . . nè* (neither . . . nor).

7.2. Subordinating conjunctions introduce dependent clauses. The most common ones are: *che* (that), *benchè* (although), *come* (as), *dove* (where), *giacchè* (inasmuch as, since), *mentre* (while), *per* (for), *perchè* (because), *quando* (when), *se* (if). The conjunction *che* (that) is never omitted in Italian, as is often done in English: *Credo che Giovanni verrà* (I think [that] John will come).

THE INTERJECTION

8.1. Some of the most common interjections in Italian and their approximate English meanings are:

ah! (ah! oh!)	*evviva!* (hurrah! long live!)
ahi! (ouch! oh dear!)	*guai!* (woe!)
ahimè! (alas!)	*oh!* (oh!)
ecco! (there!)	*viva!* (hail!)

8.2. Exclamative phrases are used as interjections:

Che bella! (How pretty!)   *Che peccato!* (What a pity!)

THE VERB

9.1 In Italian the verb has a large number of endings which differ according to subject, tense, and mood. The best way to learn the verb forms properly is in the context in which they are used.

There are three conjugations in Italian which are indicated by the ending of the infinitive:

First conjugation	*Second conjugation*	*Third conjugation*
parl-are (to speak)	**vend-ere** (to sell)	**part-ire** (to leave)

The stem of a verb is what is left after striking off the ending of the infinitive. The endings of the different moods, tenses, and persons are added to these stems.

INDICATIVE

Present

The Italian *parlo* corresponds to the English "I speak," "I am speaking," " I do speak."

First conjugation	*Second conjugation*	*Third conjugation*
io parl-*o*	vend-*o*	part-*o*
tu parl-*i*	vend-*i*	part-*i*
Lei (egli, ella) parl-*a*	vend-*e*	part-*e*
noi parl-*iamo*	vend-*iamo*	part-*iamo*
voi parl-*ate*	vend-*ete*	part-*ite*
Loro (essi, -e) parl-*ano*	vend-*ono*	part-*ono*

The pronouns *io* etc. in Italian may be omitted because the endings themselves indicate the subject. They are used when emphasis is required: *Io l'ho venduto* (I sold it). For regular verbs, all simple tenses of the indicative (except the future and the conditional) are formed by taking the stem of the verb and adding to it the endings which are printed in italics to help the student distinguish them.

The third conjugation includes a number of verbs which are characterized by the insertion of *-isc-* between the stem of the verb and the person-ending in the three persons of the singular and in the third person plural of the present indicative, the present subjunctive and the imperative, e.g. *cap-ire* (to understand); present indicative: *cap-isc-o, cap-isc-i, cap-isc-e, cap-iamo, cap-ite, cap-isc-ono;* present subjunctive: *cap-isc-a, cap-isc-a, cap-isc-a, cap-iamo, cap-iate, cap-isc-ano;* imperative: *cap-isc-a, cap-iamo, cap-isc-ano.*

Imperfect

The Italian *parlavo* corresponds to the English "I was speaking," "I used to speak" and "I spoke."

parl-*avo*	vend-*evo*	part-*ivo*
parl-*avi*	vend-*evi*	part-*ivi*
parl-*ava*	vend-*eva*	part-*iva*
parl-*avamo*	vend-*evamo*	part-*ivamo*
parl-*avate*	vend-*evate*	part-*ivate*
parl-*avano*	vend-*evano*	part-*ivano*

Future

parl-*er-ò*	vend-*er-ò*	part-*ir-ò*
parl-*er-ai*·	vend-*er-ai*	part-*ir-ai*
parl-*er-à*	vend-*er-à*	part-*ir-à*
parl-*er-emo*	vend-*er-emo*	part-*ir-emo*
parl-*er-ete*	vend-*er-ete*	part-*ir-ete*
parl-*er-anno*	vend-*er-anno*	part-*ir-anno*

Past

parl-*ai*	vend-*ei*	part-*ii*
parl-*asti*	vend-*esti*	part-*isti*
parl-*ò*	vend-*è*	part-*ì*
parl-*ammo*	vend-*emmo*	part-*immo*
parl-*aste*	vend-*este*	part-*iste*
parl-*arono*	vend-*erono*	part-*irono*

Conditional

parl*er-ei*	vend-*er-ei*	part-*ir-ei*
parl-*er-esti*	vend-*er-esti*	part-*ir-esti*
parl-*er-ebbe*	vend-*er-ebbe*	part-*ir-ebbe*
parl-*er-emmo*	vend-*er-emmo*	part-*ir-emmo*
parl-*er-este*	vend-*er-este*	part-*ir-este*
parl-*er-ebbero*	vend-*er-ebbero*	part-*ir-ebbero*

COMPOUND TENSES

All compound tenses of both the indicative and the subjunctive are formed by the proper tense of the auxiliary verbs *avere* (to have) or *essere* (to be) plus the past participle.

Many Italian verbs are conjugated with the auxiliary *avere* in the compound tenses. However, there are a number of verbs which take the auxiliary verb *essere*. The most common of these verbs are: *andare* (to go), *arrivare* or *giungere* (to arrive), *cadere* (to fall), *diventare* (to become), *entrare* (to enter), *essere* (to be), *morire* (to die), *nascere* (to be born), *partire* (to leave), *restare* (to remain), *rimanere* (to remain), *ritornare* (to return), *salire* (to go up, to climb) *scendere* (to go down, to descend), *uscire* (to go out), *venire* (to come). All the reflexive, passive and impersonal verbs take the auxiliary ESSERE.

Perfect

It is formed by the present of *avere* or *essere* plus the past participle:

ho	parlato	ho	venduto	sono	partito (-a)
hai	parlato	hai	venduto	sei	partito (-a)
ha	parlato	ha	venduto	è	partito (-a)
abbiamo	parlato	abbiamo	venduto	siamo	partiti (-e)
avete	parlato	avete	venduto	siete	partiti (-e)
hanno	parlato	hanno	venduto	sono	partiti (-e)

In Italian, the perfect is often used in cases in which the past is used in English. (See 4.7.a.)

Pluperfect

It is formed by the imperfect of *avere* or *essere* plus the past participle:

avevo	parlato	avevo	venduto	ero	partito (-a)
avevi	parlato	avevi	venduto	eri	partito (-a)
aveva	parlato	aveva	venduto	era	partito (-a)
avevamo	parlato	avevamo	venduto	eravamo	partiti (-e)
avevate	parlato	avevate	venduto	eravate	partiti (-e)
avevano	parlato	avevano	venduto	erano	partiti (-e)

Future perfect

It is formed by the future of *avere* or *essere* plus the past participle:

avrò	parlato	avrò	venduto	sarò	partito (-a)
avrai	parlato	avrai	venduto	sarai	partito (-a)
avrà	parlato	avrà	venduto	sarà	partito (-a)
avremo	parlato	avremo	venduto	saremo	partiti (-e)
avrete	parlato	avrete	venduto	sarete	partiti (-e)
avranno	parlato	avranno	venduto	saranno	partiti (-e)

SUBJUNCTIVE

9.2. The subjunctive mood is used more frequently in Italian than in English. It occurs mostly in dependent clauses when the main verb expresses uncertainty or possibility. The word "che" generally connects the two clauses and must never be omitted: *Spero che arrivi presto* (I hope [that] he arrives soon); *Suppongo che parli inglese* (I suppose [that] he speaks English).

The subjunctive is also used in dependent clauses following verbs or expressions of desire, command, fear, wonder, and similar emotions: *Temo che non venga oggi* (I fear he may not [or will not] come today); *Vuole che io l'accompagni* (He wants me to accompany him); *Sono felice che Lei sia venuto* (I'm happy you have come).

The subjunctive follows such expressions as: *bisogna* (it is necessary); *è necessario* (it is necessary); *può darsi* (it is possible); *è facile* (it is easy); *è difficile* (it is difficult); *è possibile* (it is possible); *è probabile* (it is probable); *è meglio* (it is better); *è peccato* (it is a pity); *vale la pena* (it is worth while); *pare* (it seems); *non c' è nessuno* (there is nobody); *non c' è nulla* (there is nothing); *chiunque* (whoever); *qualunque* (whatever).

The subjunctive is used after *benchè* (although), *prima che* (before), *nel caso che* (in case), *a meno che* (unless), *senza che* (without), *perchè* (provided that).

The present tense of the subjunctive is used in connection with the present or future of the indicative. (See examples above.)

The imperfect of the subjunctive is used in connection with the imperfect of the indicative: *Non c'era nessuno che parlasse inglese* (There was no one who spoke English); *Era probabile che Giovanni fosse a Roma* (It was probable that John was in Rome).

The tenses of the subjunctive are the present, imperfect, perfect and pluperfect.

Present

parl-*i*	vend-*a*	part-*a*
parl-*i*	vend-*a*	part-*a*
parl-*i*	vend-*a*	part-*a*
parl-*iamo*	vend-*iamo*	part-*iamo*
parl-*iate*	vend-*iate*	part-*iate*
parl-*ino*	vend-*ano*	part-*ano*

Imperfect

parl-*assi*	vend-*essi*	part-*issi*
parl-*assi*	vend-*essi*	part-*issi*
parl-*asse*	vend-*esse*	part-*isse*
parl-*assimo*	vend-*essimo*	part-*issimo*
parl-*aste*	vend-*este*	part-*iste*
parl-*assero*	vend-*essero*	part-*issero*

Perfect

It is formed by the present subjunctive of *avere* or *essere* plus the past participle:

abbia	parlato	abbia	venduto	sia	partito (-a)
abbia	parlato	abbia	venduto	sia	partito (-a)
abbia	parlato	abbia	venduto	sia	partito (-a)
abbiamo	parlato	abbiamo	venduto	siamo	partiti (-e)
abbiate	parlato	abbiate	venduto	siate	partiti (-e)
abbiano	parlato	abbiano	venduto	siano	partiti (-e)

Pluperfect

It is formed by the imperfect subjunctive of *avere* or *essere* plus the past participle:

avessi	parlato	avessi	venduto	fossi	partito (-a)
avessi	parlato	avessi	venduto	fossi	partito (-a)
avesse	parlato	avesse	venduto	fosse	partito (-a)
avessimo	parlato	avessimo	venduto	fossimo	partiti (-e)
aveste	parlato	aveste	venduto	foste	partiti (-e)
avessero	parlato	avessero	venduto	fossero	partiti (-e)

THE IMPERATIVE

9.3. In the imperative the polite form for the second person singular and plural is the subjunctive form of the verbs:

Parli (sing.)	*Parlino* (pl.) Speak
Venda (sing.)	*Vendano* (pl.) Sell
Parta (sing.)	*Partano* (pl.) Leave

The first person plural form is the same as that of the present tense: *parliamo* (let us speak), *vendiamo* (let us sell), *partiamo* (let us leave).

The second-person forms of the true imperative are used only within the family, in giving commands to children and to close friends:

parla (sing.)	*parlate* (pl.)
vendi (sing.)	*vendete* (pl.)
parti (sing.)	*partite* (pl.)

The negative form in the singular is the same as the infinitive: *Non parlare.*

THE PARTICIPLE

9.4. The gerund or present participle is invariable in gender and number:

First conjugation	*Second conjugation*	*Third conjugation*
parl-ando (speaking)	**vend-endo** (selling)	**part-endo** (leaving)

They are used most frequently in Italian when the English uses phrases in which "in", "by", "while" are expressed or not according to one's feeling: *Facendo così, dimenticava la regola* ([In] doing this, he was forgetting the rule); *Sbagliando, s'impara* ([By] making mistakes, one learns); *Piangeva leggendo la lettera* (He was crying [while] reading the letter).

The gerund is used as in English, to indicate manner: *Arrivò correndo* (He arrived running).

An important use of the gerund is with the verb *stare* describing vividly an action in progress: *Sto leggendo la Divina Comedia* (I am reading the *Divine Comedy*); *Stava traversando la strada* (He was crossing the street).

9.5. The past participle is inflected as an adjective: *parl-ato* (spoken), *vend-uto* (sold), *part-ito* (left). Frequently it is used in place of a whole clause, in which case it usually opens the sentence: *Venduto il libro, partì* (The book sold, he left [After he sold the book, he left]).

LIST OF IRREGULAR VERBS

9.6. The following list gives the hundred most common Italian irregular verbs. Of the simple tenses, only those which are irregular and those which might present problems in spelling are listed. Since the past participle is given, the compound tenses, which are formed with the past participle, are not included. The following abbreviations are used:

P.P.—Past Participle
PRES.—Present Indicative
P. DEF.—Past Definite
IMPF.—Imperfect Indicative
FUT.—Future

COND.—Conditional
IMPV.—Imperative
PRES. SUB.—Present Subjunctive
IMPF. SUB.—Imperfect Subjunctive

Accendere
to light
P.P. *acceso*
P. DEF. *accesi, accendesti, accese, accendemmo, accendeste, accesero*

Accogliere
to receive, to welcome
P.P. *accolto*
PRES. *accolgo, accogli, accoglie, accogliamo, accogliete, accolgono*
P. DEF. *accolsi, accogliesti, accolse, accogliemmo, accoglieste, accolsero*

Accorgersi
to notice, to perceive
P.P. *accorto*
P. DEF. *mi accorsi, ti accorgesti, si accorse, ci accorgemmo, vi accorgeste, si accorsero*

Accludere
to inclose
P.P. *accluso*
P. DEF. *acclusi, accludesti, accluse, accludemmo, accludeste, acclusero*

Affliggere
to afflict
P.P. *afflitto*
P. DEF. *afflissi, affliggesti, afflisse, affliggemmo, affliggeste, afflissero*

Andare
to go (takes auxiliary *essere*)
PRES. *vado, vai, va, andiamo, andate, vanno*
FUT. *andrò, andrai, andrà, andremo, andrete, andranno*
COND. *andrei, andresti, andrebbe, andremmo, andreste, andrebbero*
IMPV. *và, vada, andiamo, andate, vadano*

PRES. SUB. *vada, vada, vada, andiamo, andiate, vadano*

Appartenere
to belong (conjugated like *tenere*)

Appendere
to hang
P.P. *appeso*
P. DEF. *appesi, appendesti, appese, appendemmo, appendeste, appesero*

Apprendere
to learn (conjugated like *prendere*)

Aprire
to open
P.P. *aperto*
P. DEF. *aprii* or *apersi, apristi, aprì* or *aperse, aprimmo, apriste, aprirono* or *apersero*

Ardere
to burn
P.P. *arso*
P. DEF. *arsi, ardesti, arse, ardemmo, ardeste, arsero*

Avere
to have
PRES. *ho, hai, ha, abbiamo, avete, hanno*
P. DEF. *ebbi, avesti, ebbe, avemmo, aveste, ebbero*
FUT. *avrò, avrai, avrà, avremo, avrete, avranno*
COND. *avrei, avresti, avrebbe, avremmo, avreste, avrebbero*
IMPV. *abbi, abbia, abbiamo, abbiate, abbiano*
PRES. SUB. *abbia, abbia, abbia, abbiamo, abbiate, abbiano*

Bere
to drink (conjugated from the old infinitive *bevere*)

P.P. *bevuto*

P. DEF. *bevvi, bevesti, bevve, bevemmo, beveste, bevvero*

FUT. *berrò, berrai, berrà, berremo, berrete, berranno*

COND. *berrei, berresti, berrebbe, berremmo, berreste, berrebbero*

Cadere
to fall (takes auxiliary *essere*)

P. DEF. *caddi, cadesti, cadde, cademmo, cadeste, caddero*

FUT. *cadrò, cadrai, cadrà, cadremo, cadrete, cadranno*

COND. *cadrei, cadresti, cadrebbe, cadremmo, cadreste, cadrebbero*

Chiedere
to ask

P.P. *chiesto*

P. DEF. *chiesi, chiedesti, chiese, chiedemmo, chiedeste, chiesero*

Chiudere
to close

P.P. *chiuso*

P. DEF. *chiusi, chiudesti, chiuse, chiudemmo, chiudeste, chiusero*

Cogliere
to pick (flowers, etc.), to gather

P.P. *colto*

P. DEF. *colsi, cogliesti, colse, cogliemmo, coglieste, colsero*

Compiere or Compire
to accomplish, to finish

P.P. *compito* or *compiuto*

PRES. *compio, compi, compie, compiamo, compite, compiono;* also *compisco, compisci, compisce, compiamo, compite, compiscono*

FUT. *compirò, compirai, compirà, compiremo, compirete, compiranno*

COND. *compirei, compiresti, compirebbe, compiremmo, compireste, compirebbero*

IMPV. *compi, compia, compiamo, compite, compiano*

PRES. SUB. *compia, compia, compia, compiamo, compiate, compiano;* also *compisca, compisca, compisca, compiamo, compiate, compiscano*

Concedere
to grant, to concede

P.P. *concesso*

P. DEF. *concessi, concedesti, concesse, concedemmo, concedeste, concessero*

Condurre
to lead, to conduct (conjugated from old infinitive *conducere*)

P.P. *condotto*

PRES. GERUND. *conducendo*

PRES. *conduco, conduci, conduce; conduciamo, conducete, conducono*

IMPF. *conducevo, conducevi, conduceva, conducevamo, conducevate, conducevano*

P. DEF. *condussi, conducesti, condusse, conducemmo, conduceste, condussero*

FUT. *condurrò, condurrai, condurrà, condurremo, condurrete, condurranno*

COND. *condurrei, condurresti, condurrebbe, condurremmo, condurreste, condurrebbero*

IMPF. *conduci, conduca, conduciamo, conducete, conducano*

PRES. SUB. *conduca, conduca, conduca, conduciamo, conduciate, conducano*

IMPF. SUB. *conducessi, conducessi, conducesse, conducessimo, conduceste, conducessero*

Conoscere
to know (usually a person)

P.P. *conosciuto*

P. DEF. *conobbi, conoscesti, conobbe, conoscemmo, conosceste, conobbero*

Coprire
to cover

P.P. *coperto*

Correggere
to correct

P.P. *corretto*

P. DEF. *corressi, correggesti, corresse, correggemmo, correggeste, corressero*

Correre
to run (conjugated with *essere* when it means from one place to another, otherwise it is conjugated with *avere*)

P.P. *corso*

P. DEF. *corsi, corresti, corse, corremmo, correste, corsero*

Crescere
to grow (conjugated with *essere* except when it has a direct object)

P.P. *cresciuto*

P. DEF. *crebbi, crescesti, crebbe, crescemmo, cresceste, crebbero*

Cuocere
to cook
P.P. *cotto*
PRES. *cuocio, cuoci, cuoce, cuociamo (cociamo), cuocete (cocete), cuociono*
P. DEF. *cossi, cocesti, cosse, cuocemmo, cuoceste, cossero*
PRES. SUB. *cuocia, cuocia, cuocia, cuociamo, cuociate, cuociano*

Dare
to give
P.P. *dato*
PRES. *do, dai, dà, diamo, date, danno*
P. DEF. *diedi, desti, diede, demmo, deste, diedero*
IMPF. *davo, davi, dava, davamo, davate, davano*
FUT. *darò, darai, darà, daremo, darete, daranno*
COND. *darei, daresti, darebbe, daremmo, dareste, darebbero*
IMPV. *dà, dia, diamo, date, diano*
PRES. SUB. *dia, dia, dia, diamo, diate, diano*
IMPF. SUB. *dessi, dessi, desse, dessimo, deste, dessero*

Decidere
to decide
P.P. *deciso*
P. DEF. *decisi, decidesti, decise, decidemmo, decideste, decisero*

Difendere
to defend
P.P. *difeso*
P. DEF. *difesi, difendesti, difese, difendemmo, difendeste, difesero*

Dipingere
to paint
P.P. *dipinto*
P. DEF. *dipinsi, dipingesti, dipinse, dipingemmo, dipingeste, dipinsero*

Dire
to say, to tell
(conjugated from old infinitive *dicere*)
P.P. *detto*
PRES. GERUND. *dicendo*
PRES. *dico, dici, dice, diciamo, dite, dicono*
P. DEF. *dissi, dicesti, disse, dicemmo, diceste, dissero*
IMPF. *dicevo, dicevi, diceva, dicevamo, dicevate, dicevano*
FUT. *dirò, dirai, dirà, diremo, direte, diranno*
COND. *direi, diresti, direbbe, diremmo, direste, direbbero*
IMPV. *di'* (or *dici*), *dica, diciamo, dite, dicano*

PRES. SUB. *dica, dica, dica, diciamo, diciate, dicano*
IMPF. SUB. *dicessi, dicessi, dicesse, dicessimo, diceste, dicessero*

Dirigere
to direct
P.P. *diretto*
P. DEF. *diressi, dirigesti, diresse, dirigemmo, dirigeste, diressero*

Discutere
to discuss
P.P. *discusso*
P. DEF. *discussi, discutesti, discusse, discutemmo, discuteste, discussero*

Dividere
to divide
P.P. *diviso*
P. DEF. *divisi, dividesti, divise, dividemmo, divideste, divisero*

Dovere
to have to, must
P.P. *dovuto*
PRES. *devo* (or *debbo*), *devi, deve, dobbiamo, dovete, devono* (or *debbono*)
P. DEF. *dovei* (or *dovetti*), *dovesti, dovè* (or *dovette*), *dovemmo, doveste, doverono* (or *dovettero*)
FUT. *dovrò, dovrai, dovrà, dovremo, dovrete, dovranno*
COND. *dovrei, dovresti, dovrebbe, dovremmo, dovreste, dovrebbero*
PRES. SUB. *deva, deva, deva* (or *debba, debba, debba*), *dobbiamo, dobbiate, devano* (or *debbano*)

Esprimere
to express
P.P. *espresso*
P. DEF. *espressi, esprimesti, espresse, esprimemmo, esprimeste, espressero*

Essere
to be (conjugated with itself as auxiliary)
P.P. *stato*
PRES. *sono, sei, è, siamo, siete, sono*
P. DEF. *fui, fosti, fu, fummo, foste, furono*
IMPF. *ero, eri, era, eravamo, eravate, erano*
FUT. *sarò, sarai, sarà, saremo, sarete, saranno*
COND. *sarei, saresti, sarebbe, saremmo, sareste, sarebbero*
IMPV. *sii, sia, siamo, siate, siano*
PRES. SUB. *sia, sia, sia, siamo, siate, siano*
IMPF. SUB. *fossi, fossi, fosse, fossimo, foste, fossero*

Fare
to do, to make (conjugated from the old infinitive *facere*)

P.P. *fatto*
PRES. GERUND. *facendo*
PRES. *faccio, fai, fa, facciamo, fate, fanno*
P. DEF. *feci, facesti, fece, facemmo, faceste, fecero*
IMPF. *facevo, facevi, faceva, facevamo, facevate, facevano*
FUT. *farò, farai, farà, faremo, farete, faranno*
COND. *farei, faresti, farebbe, faremmo, fareste, farebbero*
IMPV. *fà, faccia, facciamo, fate, facciano*
PRES. SUB. *faccia, faccia, faccia, facciamo, facciate, facciano*
IMPF. SUB. *facessi, facessi, facesse, facessimo, faceste, facessero*

Fingere
to pretend, to feign

P.P. *finto*
P. DEF. *finsi, fingesti, finse, fingemmo, fingeste, finsero*

Giungere
to arrive, to reach (conjugated with *essere*)

P.P. *giunto*
P. DEF. *giunsi, giungesti, giunse, giungemmo, giungeste, giunsero*

Leggere
to read

P.P. *letto*
P. DEF. *lessi, leggesti, lesse, leggemmo, leggeste, lessero*

Mantenere
to maintain, to keep, to support (conjugated like *tenere*)

Mettere
to put

P.P. *messo*
P. DEF. *misi, mettesti, mise, mettemmo, metteste, misero*

Mordere
to bite

P.P. *morso*
P. DEF. *morsi, mordesti, morse, mordemmo, mordeste, morsero*

Morire
to die (conjugated with *essere*)

P.P. *morto*
PRES. *muoio, muori, muore, moriamo, morite, muoiono*
FUT. *morrò, morrai, morrà, morremo, morrete, morranno*
COND. *morrei, morresti, morrebbe, morremmo, morreste, morrebbero*
NOTE: The regular forms for the future and conditional are also used.
IMPV. *muori, muoia, moriamo, morite, muoiano*
PRES. SUB. *muoia, muoia, muoia, moriamo, moriate, muoiano*

Muovere
to move (*not* to change residence)

P.P. *mosso*
PRES. *muovo, muovi, muove, moviamo, movete, muovono*
P. DEF. *mossi, movesti, mosse, movemmo, moveste, mossero*
IMPV. *muovi, muova, moviamo, movete, muovano*
PRES. SUB. *muova, muova, muova, moviamo, moviate, muovano*

Nascere
to be born (conjugated with *essere*)

P.P. *nato*
P. DEF. *egli nacque, essi nacquero*

Nascondere
to hide, to conceal

P.P. *nascosto*
P. DEF. *nascosi, nascondesti, nascose, nascondemmo, nascondeste, nascosero*

Offendere
to offend

P.P. *offeso*
P. DEF. *offesi, offendesti, offese, offendemmo, offendeste, offesero*

Offrire
to offer

P.P. *offerto*
P. DEF. *offrii* (or *offersi*), *offristi, offrì* (or *offerse*), *offrimmo, offriste, offrirono* (or *offersero*)

Perdere
to lose

P.P. *perduto* or *perso*
P. DEF. *persi* (or *perdei* or *perdetti*), *perdesti, perse* (or *perdè* or *perdette*), *perdemmo, perdeste, persero* (or *perderono* or *perdettero*)

Persuadere
to persuade

P.P. *persuaso*
P. DEF. *persuasi, persuadesti, persuase, persuademmo, persuadeste, persuasero*

Piacere
to like, to please, to be pleasing (conjugated with *essere*)
NOTE: This verb is used mostly in the third person singular and plural.

P.P. *piaciuto*
PRES. *piaccio, piaci, piace, piacciamo, piacete, piacciono*
P. DEF. *piacqui, piacesti, piacque, piacemmo, piaceste, piacquero*
PRES. SUB. *piaccia, piaccia, piaccia, piacciamo, piacciate, piacciano*

Piangere
to cry, to weep

P.P. *pianto*
P. DEF. *piansi, piangesti, pianse, piangemmo, piangeste, piansero*

Porre (Ponere)
to put, to place

P.P. *posto*
PRES. GERUND. *ponendo*
PRES. *pongo, poni, pone, poniamo, ponete, pongono*
P. DEF. *posi, ponesti, pose, ponemmo, poneste, posero*
FUT. *porrò, porrai, porrà, porremo, porrete, porranno*
COND. *porrei, porresti, porrebbe, porremmo, porreste, porrebbero*
IMPF. *ponevo, ponevi, poneva, ponevamo, ponevate, ponevano*
IMPV. *poni, ponga, poniamo, ponete, pongano*
PRES. SUB. *ponga, ponga, ponga, poniamo, poniate, pongano*
IMPF. SUB. *ponessi, ponessi, ponesse, ponessimo, poneste, ponessero*

Potere
to be able to, can, may

PRES. *posso, puoi, può, possiamo, potete, possono*
FUT. *potrò, potrai, potrà, potremo, potrete, potranno*
COND. *potrei, potresti, potrebbe, potremmo, potreste, potrebbero*
IMPV. *possa, possa, possiamo, possiate, possano*
PRES. SUB. *possa, possa, possa, possiamo, possiate, possano*

Prendere
to take

P.P. *preso*
P. DEF. *presi, prendesti, prese, prendemmo, prendeste, presero*

Produrre
to produce (conjugated like *condurre*)

Proteggere
to protect

P.P. *protetto*
P. DEF. *protessi, proteggesti, protesse, proteggemmo, proteggeste, protessero*

Radere
to shave

P.P. *raso*
P. DEF. *rasi, redesti, rase, rademmo, radeste, rasero*

Rendere
to render, to give back

P.P. *reso*
P. DEF. *resi, rendesti, rese, rendemmo, rendeste, resero*

Ridere
to laugh

P.P. *riso*
P. DEF. *risi, ridesti, rise, ridemmo, rideste, risero*

Rimanere
to remain

P.P. *rimasto*
PRES. *rimango, rimani, rimane, rimaniamo, rimanete, rimangono*
P. DEF. *rimasi, rimanesti, rimase, rimanemmo, rimaneste, rimasero*
FUT. *rimarrò, rimarrai, rimarrà, rimarremo, rimarrete, rimarranno*
COND. *rimarrei, rimarresti, rimarrebbe, rimarremmo, rimarreste, rimarrebbero*
IMPV. *rimani, rimanga, rimaniamo, rimanete, rimangano*
PRES. SUB. *rimanga, rimanga, rimanga, rimaniamo, rimaniate, rimangano*

Rispondere
to answer, to reply

P.P. *risposto*
P. DEF. *risposi, rispondesti, rispose, rispondemmo, rispondeste, risposero*

Ritenere
to retain (conjugated like *tenere*)

Rompere
to break

P.P. *rotto*

P. DEF. *ruppi, rompesti, ruppe, rompemmo, rompeste, ruppero*

Salire
to go up, to climb, to ascend, to get on

PRES. *salgo, sali, sale, saliamo, salite, salgono*

IMPV. *sali, salga, saliamo, salite, salgano*

PRES. SUB. *salga, salga, salga, saliamo, saliate, salgano*

Sapere
to know, to know how (*never* to know a person)

PRES. *so, sai, sa, sappiamo, sapete, sanno*

P. DEF. *seppi, sapesti, seppe, sapemmo, sapeste, seppero*

FUT. *saprò, saprai, saprà, sapremo, saprete, sapranno*

COND. *saprei, sapresti, saprebbe, sapremmo, sapreste, saprebbero*

IMPV. *sappi, sappia, sappiamo, sappiate, sappiano*

PRES. SUB. *sappia, sappia, sappia, sappiamo, sappiate, sappiano*

Scegliere
to choose, to select

P.P. *scelto*

PRES. *scelgo, scegli, sceglie, scegliamo, scegliete, scelgono*

P. DEF. *scelsi, scegliesti, scelse, scegliemmo, sceglieste, scelsero*

IMPV. *scegli, scelga, scegliamo, scegliete, scelgano*

PRES. SUB. *scelga, scelga, scelga, scegliamo, scegliate, scelgano*

Scendere
to descend, to go down, to get down, to get off

P.P. *sceso*

P. DEF. *scesi, scendesti, scese, scendemmo, scendeste, scesero*

Sciogliere
to untie, to dissolve, to melt

P.P. *sciolto*

P. DEF. *sciolsi, sciogliesti, sciolse, sciogliemmo, scioglieste, sciolsero*

IMPV. *sciogli, sciolga, sciogliamo, sciogliete, sciolgano*

PRES. SUB. *sciolga, sciolga, sciolga, sciogliamo, sciogliate, sciolgano*

Scomparire
to disappear

P.P. *scomparso* or *scomparito*

PRES. *scompaio, scompari, scompare, scompariamo, scomparite, scompaiono*

P. DEF. *scomparii (or scomparvi or scomparsi), scomparisti, scomparì (or scomparve or scomparse), scomparimmo, scompariste, scomparirono (or scomparvero or scomparsero)*

IMPV. *scompari, scompaia, scompariamo, scomparite, scompaiano*

PRS. SUB. *scompaia, scompaia, scompaia, scompariamo, scompariate, scompaiano*

NOTE: Besides the forms given above, this verb also has the regular -*isco* forms in the present indicative, imperative, and present subjunctive.

Scoprire
to discover

P.P. *scoperto*

P. DEF. *scoprii (or scopersi), scopristi, scoprì (or scoperse), scoprimmo, scopriste, scoprirono (or scopersero)*

Scrivere
to write

P.P. *scritto*

P. DEF. *scrissi, scrivesti, scrisse, scrivemmo, scriveste, scrissero*

Sedere
to sit

PRES. *siedo (or seggo), siedi, siede, sediamo, sedete, siedono (or seggono)*

IMPV. *siedi, segga, sediamo, sedete, seggano*

PRES. SUB. *segga, segga, segga (or sieda, sieda, sieda), sediamo, sediate, seggano (or siedano)*

Soffrire
to suffer

P.P. *sofferto*

P. DEF. *soffrii (or soffersi), soffristi, soffrì (or sofferse), soffrimmo, soffriste, soffrirono (or soffersero)*

Sorgere
to arise, to rise

P.P. *sorto*

P. DEF. *sorsi, sorgesti, sorse, sorgemmo, sorgeste, sorsero*

Sorridere
to smile (conjugated like *ridere*)

Spargere
to spread, to scatter
P.P. *sparso*
P. DEF. *sparsi, spargesti, sparse, spargemmo, spargeste, sparsero*

Spegnere or **Spengere**
to extinguish
P.P. *spento*
PRES. (regular) also *io spengo, essi spengono*
P. DEF. *spensi, spegnesti, spense, spegnemmo, spegneste, spensero*
IMPV. *spegni, spenga, spegniamo, spegnete, spengano*
PRES. SUB. *spenga, spenga, spenga, spegniamo, spegniate, spengano*

Spendere
to spend
P.P. *speso*
P. DEF. *spesi, spendesti, spese, spendemmo, spendeste, spesero*

Spingere
to push, to shove, to thrust
P.P. *spinto*
P. DEF. *spinsi, spingesti, spinse, spingemmo, spingeste, spinsero*

Stare
to stay (sometimes, to be, to stand) (conjugated with *essere*)
P.P. *stato*
PRES. *sto, stai, sta, stiamo, state, stanno*
P. DEF. *stetti, stesti, stette, stemmo, steste, stettero*
IMPF. *stavo, stavi, stava, stavamo, stavate, stavano*
FUT. *starò, starai, starà, staremo, starete, staranno*
COND. *starei, staresti, starebbe, staremmo, stareste, starebbero*
IMPV. *stà, stia, stiamo, state, stiano*
PRES. SUB. *stia, stia, stia, stiamo, stiate, stiano*
IMPF. SUB. *stessi, stessi, stesse, stessimo, steste, stessero*

Stringere
to hold fast, to squeeze, to grasp, to bind fast
P.P. *stretto*
P. DEF. *strinsi, stringesti, strinse, stringemmo, stringeste, strinsero*

Supporre
to suppose (conjugated like *porre*)

Svenire
to faint (conjugated like *venire;* takes the auxiliary *essere*)

Tacere
to be silent, to keep quiet
P.P. *taciuto*
PRES. *taccio, taci, tace, taciamo, tacete, tacciono*
P. DEF. *tacqui, tacesti, tacque, tacemmo, taceste, tacquero*
IMPV. *taci, taccia, taciamo, tacete, tacciano*
PRES. SUB. *taccia, taccia, taccia, tacciamo, tacciate, tacciano*
(may also be written with one *c*)

Tenere
to hold, to have, to keep
PRES. *tengo, tieni, tiene, teniamo, tenete, tengono*
P. DEF. *tenni, tenesti, tenne, tenemmo, teneste, tennero*
FUT. *terrò, terrai, terrà, terremo, terrete, terranno*
COND. *terrei, terresti, terrebbe, terremmo, terreste, terrebbero*
IMPV. *tieni, tenga, teniamo, tenete, tengano*
PRES. SUB. *tenga, tenga, tenga, teniamo, teniate, tengano*

Togliere
to take away, to remove, to take from
P.P. *tolto*
PRES. *tolgo, togli, toglie, togliamo, togliete, tolgono*
P. DEF. *tolsi, togliesti, tolse, togliemmo, toglieste, tolsero*
FUT. *torrò, torrai, torrà, torremo, torrete, torranno*
COND. *torrei, torresti, torrebbe, torremmo, torreste, torrebbero*
NOTE: Both the future and the conditional have the regular forms in addition to those given above.
IMPV. *togli, tolga, togliamo, togliete, tolgano*
PRES. SUB. *tolga, tolga, tolga, togliamo, togliate, tolgano*

Tradurre
to translate (from the old infinitive *traducere;* conjugated like *condurre*)

Trarre
to draw or pull out; to drag, to haul, to derive

P.P. *tratto*

PRES. GERUND. *traendo*

PRES. *traggo, trai, trae, traiamo, traete, traggono*

P. DEF. *trassi, traesti, trasse, traemmo, traeste, trassero*

IMPF. *traevo, traevi, traeva, traevamo, traevate, traevano*

FUT. *trarrò, trarrai, trarrà, trarremo, trarrete, trarranno*

COND. *trarrei, trarresti, trarrebbe, trarremmo, trarreste, trarrebbero*

IMPV. *trai, tragga, traiamo, traete, traggano*

PRES. SUB. *tragga, tragga, tragga, traiamo, traiate, traggano*

IMPF. SUB. *traessi, traessi, traesse, traessimo, traeste, traessero*

Uccidere
to kill

P.P. *ucciso*

P. DEF. *uccisi, uccidesti, uccise, uccidemmo, uccideste, uccisero*

Udire
to hear

PRES. *odo, odi, ode, udiamo, udite, odono*

FUT. *udrò, udrai, udrà, udremo, udrete, udranno*

COND. *udrei, udresti, udrebbe, udremmo, udreste, udrebbero*

NOTE: Both the future and the conditional have regular forms in addition to those given above.

IMPV. *odi, oda, udiamo, udite, odano*

PRES. SUB. *oda, oda, oda, udiamo, udiate, odano*

Uscire
to go out (takes the auxiliary *essere*)

PRES. *esco, esci, esce, usciamo, uscite, escono*

IMPV. *esci, esca, usciamo, uscite, escano*

PRES. SUB. *esca, esca, esca, usciamo, usciate, escano*

Valere
to be worth (takes the auxiliary *essere*)

P.P. *valso*

PRES. *valgo, vali, vale, valiamo, valete, valgono*

P. DEF. *valsi, valesti, valse, valemmo, valeste, valsero*

FUT. *varrò, varrai, varrà, varremo, varrete, varranno*

COND. *varrei, varresti, varrebbe, varremmo, varrete, varrebbero*

IMPV. *vali, valga, valiamo, valete, valgano*

PRES. SUB. *valga, valga, valga, valiamo, valiate, valgano*

NOTE: Of this verb usually only the third person singular and the third person plural are used.

Vedere
to see

P.P. *visto* or *veduto*

P. DEF. *vidi, vedesti, vide, vedemmo, vedeste, videro*

FUT. *vedrò, vedrai, vedrà, vedremo, vedrete, vedranno*

COND. *vedrei, vedresti, vedrebbe, vedremmo, vedreste, vedrebbero*

Venire
to come (conjugated with the auxiliary *essere*)

P.P. *venuto*

PRES. *vengo, vieni, viene, veniamo, venite, vengono*

P. DEF. *venni, venisti, venne, venimmo, veniste, vennero*

FUT. *verrò, verrai, verrà, verremo, verrete, verranno*

COND. *verrei, verresti, verrebbe, verremmo, verreste, verrebbero*

IMPV. *vieni, venga, veniamo, venite, vengano*

PRES. SUB. *venga, venga, venga, veniamo, veniate, vengano*

Vincere
to win

P.P. *vinto*

P. DEF. *vinsi, vincesti, vinse, vincemmo, vinceste, vinsero*

Vivere
to live (*not* to reside)

NOTE: Takes the auxiliary *avere* if followed by a direct object, otherwise it takes the auxiliary *essere*.

P.P. *vissuto*

P. DEF. *vissi, vivesti, visse, vivemmo, viveste, vissero*

FUT. *vivrò, vivrai, vivrà, vivremo, vivrete, vivranno*

COND. *vivrei, vivresti, vivrebbe, vivremmo, vivreste, vivrebbero*

Volere
to want, to be willing, to desire, to wish

PRES. *voglio, vuoi, vuole, vogliamo, volete, vogliono*
P. DEF. *volli, volesti, volle, volemmo, voleste, vollero*
FUT. *vorrò, vorrai, vorrà, vorremo, vorrete, vorranno*
COND. *vorrei, vorresti, vorrebbe, vorremmo, vorreste, vorrebbero*
IMPV. (rarely used) *vogli, voglia, vogliamo, vogliate, vogliano*
PRES. SUB. *voglia, voglia, voglia, vogliamo, vogliate, vogliano*

Volgere
to turn, to revolve

P.P. *volto*
PRES. *volgo, volgi, volge, volgiamo, volgete, volgono*
P. DEF. *volsi, volgesti, volse, volgemmo, volgeste, volsero*

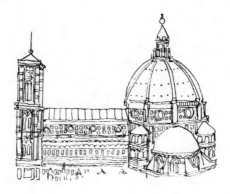

Italian-English
Dictionary*

A

a to, at
abbastanza enough
abbondanza abundance
abbracciare to embrace
abitante *m.* inhabitant
abitare to live, reside, dwell
abito suit
   . . . a giacca tailored suit (for a woman)
abituato accustomed
abitudine *f.* habit
accanto beside
accettare to accept
accendere to light
accidempoli! the deuce!
accidente accident
accogliere to receive, to welcome
accomodarsi to make oneself comfortable
accompagnare to accompany
accontentato satisfied
aceto vinegar
acqua water
acquaio kitchen sink
acquazzone *m.* shower (rain)
acquistare to acquire, to purchase
addio goodbye, farewell
addolorato grieved
addormentarsi to fall asleep

adesso now
adorare to adore
adorata beloved
aereo, in by plane
aeroplano airplane
aeroporto airport
affari *m. pl.* business
   fare . . . to do business
affascinare to fascinate
affatto at all
affittare to rent
affluenza influx
affollato crowded
affresco (*pl.* affreschi) fresco
agente *m.* agent, policeman
agenzia agency
aggiungere to add
agnello lamb
ago needle
agosto August
agricoltura agriculture
aiuto help
albergo hotel
albero tree
alberato tree lined
alcuni,-e some
alba dawn
alcuno,-a any
allarmare to alarm
   non si alarmi don't get alarmed

*In the Italian-English and English-Italian dictionaries that follow, parts of speech are not indicated except in ambiguous cases. In the case of nouns, gender is indicated only where the form of the noun does not clearly indicate masculine (*m.*) or feminine (*f.*). Irregular plurals (*pl.*) of nouns are also given. The abbreviations *adj.* for adjective and *adv.* for adverb are used where it is necessary to distinguish these parts of speech. Familiar forms are abbreviated *fam.*, polite forms, *pol.*

allegramente cheerfully
allegrezza cheerfulness
alloggiare to stay, to lodge
alloggio lodging
allora then
almeno at least
alquanto somewhat, rather
alto high, tall
altro other, else
altrui others, of others
alzare to lift, raise
alzarsi to get up
amante lover
amare to love
amaro bitter
ambedue both
americano American
amicizia friendship
amico friend
ammalarsi to get sick
ammirare to admire
amministrare to manage
ammiratore *m.* admirer
ammobiliato furnished
ammontare amount
amore love
  amor mio my love
analogo matching
ananasso pineapple
anatomico anatomist
anche also, too
ancora yet, still
  non ... not yet
andare to go
andata e ritorno round trip
angolo corner
anima soul
animale *m.* animal
anno year
annunciare announce
ansia anxiety
ansioso anxious, eager
antichità antiquity
anticipo, in in advance
antico ancient
antipasto appetizer
apostolo apostle
appagato satisfied
apparecchiare to set
apparire to appear
appartamento apartment
appassionato full of feeling

appena as soon as
appetito appetite
  avere ... to be hungry
apprezzare to appreciate
approvare approve
appuntamento appointment
aprile *m.* April
aprire to open
arachidi peanuts
arancia (*pl.* arance) orange
architetto architect
architettura architecture
ardere to burn
argenteria silverware
Argentina Argentina
argento silver
aria air
  corrente d' ... draft
  un soffio d' ... a breath of air
arrabbiato angry
arrivo arrival
armadio closet
arredare to furnish
arrivare to arrive
arrivederci until we meet again
  (*fam.*)
arrivederla until we meet again
  (*pol.*)
arrostito roasted
arrosto roast
arte *f.* art
artista *m. & f.* artist
articolo article
artistico artistic
ascensore *m.* elevator
ascesa, in rising
asciugamano towel
aspettare to wait
  ... oltre to wait any longer
  ... a lungo to wait a long time
assaggiare to taste
asino donkey
assediato besieged
assegno check
  libretto di assegni check book
assicurare to assure, to insure
assistere to attend
assolutamente absolutely
assortimento assortment
astronomo astronomer
Atene Athens
attento! careful!

atterrare to land
attesa waiting
attraente attractive
attrazione *f.* attraction
attuale present, actual
audacia audacity
augurare to wish
auguri *m. pl.* good wishes
autentico authentic
autista chauffeur, driver
autobus *m.* bus
automobile *f.* automobile, car
autorità authority
autore *m.* author
autunno autumn, fall
avanti forward, ahead
avere to have
aviazione *f.* aviation
avverarsi to come true
avvertire to warn
avvicinarsi to draw near, approach
avvolgere to wrap
azione *f.* action
azzurro blue

B

baciare to kiss
bacio kiss
bagaglio baggage
bagno bathroom, bath
  fare il ... to bathe
  fare i bagni to go bathing
ballo dance
  da ... for dancing
bambino,-a child
banana banana
banca bank
bandiera banner, flag
barca boat
barometro barometer
basilica basilica
basso low, short
battaglia battle
battere to strike, beat, knock
baule *m.* trunk
bel, bella, bello beautiful
belga Belgian
Belgio Belgium
bellezza beauty
benchè although

bene well
  sto ... I am well, I feel well
benedire to bless
benedizione *f.* blessing
beninteso of course
benone very well
bere to drink
berretto cap
biancheria linens
  ... intima underwear
bianco white
biblioteca library
bicchiere *m.* glass
bicicletta bicycle
biglietteria ticket window
biglietto ticket
  ... di visita visiting card
biondo blond
bisogna che it is necessary
bisogno need
  ho ... di I need
bistecca steak
bizzarria whim
bizzarro whimsical
bollire to boil
bollito boiled
bollo stamp, rubber stamp
bontà kindness
bordo, a on board
borsa stock exchange, scholarship
borsetta handbag
bosco woods
bottega (*pl.* botteghe) shop, store
bottiglia bottle
bottone *m.* button
braccio (*pl.* le braccia) arm
Brasile *m.* Brazil
bravo! bravissimo! fine! excellent!
breve brief, short
  a ... scadenza short term
brillante brilliant, sparkling
brodo soup
brutto ugly
bugia lie
bue *m.* beef, ox
buio dark
buono good
buon'ora, di early
burro butter
busta envelope

C

cabina cabin
caduta fall
caffè coffee
caffelatte coffee with milk
caffettiera coffee pot
calamaio inkwell
calcolo calculation
caldo hot, warm
  fa ... it is warm, hot
calendario calendar
calosce *f. pl.* overshoes, rubbers
calza stocking
calzatura footwear
calzino sock
calzoni *m. pl.* trousers, pants
cambio rate of exchange
cameriere *m.* waiter
camera room, chamber
  ... da letto bedroom
camicetta blouse
camicia (*pl.* camicie) shirt
cammin facendo on the way
cammino path, walk
campanello doorbell, small bell
campo field
Canadà *m.* Canada
canale *m.* canal
cane *m.* dog
canterellando humming
cantare to sing
canzone *f.* song
canzonetta popular song
capelli hair
capire to understand
capitale *f.* capital (of a country)
  m. capital (money)
capitano captain
capo head
capolavoro masterpiece
cappella chapel
cappello hat
carabiniere *m.* military policeman
caraffa decanter, pitcher
carbone *m.* coal
caricare to load, to wind (a watch)
carne *f.* meat
caro dear, expensive
carriera career
carrozza railroad car, carriage

carta paper
  foglio di ... sheet of paper
  ... da lettere letter paper
  ... geografica map
  ... sugante blotter
cartoleria stationary store
casa house
caserma barracks
cassettone *m.* the bureau
  (furniture)
cassiere *m.* cashier
castagna chestnut
castrato mutton
catacombe catacombs
cattedrale *f.* cathedral
cattivo bad
  fa ... tempo the weather is bad
cattolico catholic
cavallo horse
c'è there is
Ceco-slovacchia Czechoslovakia
cedere to yield, to cede
celebrare celebrate
celeste blue
cena supper
cenare to have supper
centesimo cent
centigrado centigrade
centinaia *f. pl.* hundreds
centinaio about a hundred
cento one hundred
centrale central
centro center
cera appearance, look
  avere buona ... to look well
cercare to look for, seek
  ... di to try to
cereale *m.* cereal
certamente certainly
certo certain, certainly
cesta basket
che who, that, whom, which, what,
  what a, than
  non (verb) ... only
che cosa? what?
chi who, whom
chiamare to call
chiamarsi to be called (name)
chiarore *m.* light
chiave *f.* key
chiedere to ask
chiesa church

chilo kilogram
chilogrammo kilogram
chilometro kilometer
chiudere to close
chiunque whoever
ci there; us, to us
cibo food
cima summit, top
cimitero cemetery
cinema *m.* motion picture theater
cintura belt, waist
cinquanta fifty
cinque five
ciò that
  dopo di ... after that
cioccolata chocolate
cioè that is, that is to say
cipria powder
circa about
circolazione *f.* currency, circulation
città city
civiltà civilization
classe *f.* class
clima *m.* climate
clinica doctor's office, clinic
cognata sister-in-law
cognato brother-in-law
colazione *f.* breakfast
colle *m.* hill
colletto collar
collina hill
collo neck
colore *m.* color
coltello knife
comandante *m.* commander
come as, like
cominciare to begin
comico funny
commerciale commercial
commerciante *m.* merchant
commercio trade, commerce
commosso moved, touched
commovente moving, touching
comodino night table
comodo comfortable
  quando le fa ... whenever it
  suits you
compagnia company
completamente completely
completo complete
compone, si is composed
compositore *m.* composer

composto composed
comprare to buy
con with
concedere to grant
  ti sarà concesso it will be granted
  to you
concerto concert
conciliazione *f.* conciliation
condimento seasoning
condito seasoned
condizione *f.* condition
confessare to confess
conforto comfort
congelare to freeze
connazionale *m.* fellow countryman
conoscenza acquaintance,
  knowledge
  fare la ... to make the
  acquaintance
conoscere to know
conoscitore *m.* connoisseur
consegnare to deliver
conservare to keep, preserve
  ... agli atti to keep on record
consigliare to advise
consiglio advice
consistere di to consist of
contabilità accounting
contadino peasant
contanti, in for cash
contare to count
contento glad
conto check, bill
contorno side dish
contrada quarter, section, (of a city)
contrario opposite, contrary
  al ... on the other hand, on the
  contrary
contro against
controllo della dogana customs
  inspection
convincere to convince
conversazione *f.* conversation
convinto convinced
coperta blanket
  sopra ... on deck
coperto cover, place setting
copia copy, duplicate
  in duplice ... in duplicate
coppia couple
coprire to cover
coraggio courage

corpo body
correre to run
corrispondenza correspondence
  sbrigare la ... to write the
  correspondence
corsa race
  fare una ... to run a race
corso boulevard, course
cortesia courtesy
cortile *m.* courtyard, inner court
corto short
così thus, so
cosparso strewn
costa coast
costare to cost
costoletta chop
costruire to construct, build
costume *m.* costume, custom
cotone *m.* cotton
cotto cooked
  ben ... well done, well cooked
cravatta necktie
creatura creature
creazione *f.* creation
credenza buffet
credere to believe
credito credit
  a ... on credit
crema cream
  ... a base d'olio cold cream
crescere to grow
crespo crepe
cristianesimo Christianity
Cristo Christ
crollare to collapse, to fall to pieces
crudo raw
cucchiaio spoon
cucchiaino teaspoon
cucina kitchen
cucinare to cook
cucire to sew
cucitura seam, sewing
cugino,-a cousin
cultura culture
cuoio leather
cuore *m.* heart
  nel ... della città in the center of
  the city
cupo deep dark (in ref. to a color)
cupola cupola
cuscino pillow

D

da from
danaro money
dappertutto everywhere
dare to give
  ... su to face, open upon
davanti in front
davvero really
decadenza decadence
decidere to decide
decimo tenth
decisione *f.* decision
decollare to take off (aviation)
definire to define
delizioso delicious
denaro money
dente *f.* tooth
dentifricio toothpaste
dentista *m. & f.* dentist
dentro inside
depositare to deposit, check
deposito di bagagli checkroom
  (for baggage)
descrivere to describe
descrizione *f.* description
desiderare to wish, to desire
desideroso desirous
destra, a to the right
destramente expertly, skillfully
detenuto prisoner
dettagliato detailed
devo I must
di of
diamante *m.* diamond
dicembre *m.* December
dichiarare to declare
diciotto eighteen
diciannove nineteen
diciassette seventeen
dieci ten
diecina about ten
dietro behind
differente different
differenza difference
difficile difficult
difficoltà difficulty
Dio God
dimenticare to forget
dimostrare to show
dipingere to paint
dire to say, tell

direttamente directly
direttore *m.* director
dirigente *m.* manager
disastro disaster
discesa, in dropping
discutere to discuss
disopra, al above
disotto, al below
dispiacere to displease
dispiace, mi I am sorry
disposizione *f.* disposition
 a sua . . . at your service
disposto disposed
distante distant
distanza distance
distinguere to distinguish
disturbare to bother, to disturb
disturbo bother, disturbance
dito (*pl.* le dita) finger
ditta *f.* firm
divano sofa
diventare become
diversi several
diverso different
 diverse volte several times
divertente amusing
divertimento amusement
dividere divide
divinamente divinely
dizionario dictionary
doccia shower (bath)
dodici twelve
dogana customs house
doganiere *m.* customs officer
dolce *adj.* sweet; *n. m.* dessert
dollaro dollar
dolore *m.* pain, ache
doloroso painful
domandare to ask
domani tomorrow
domenica Sunday
domestica maid
domicilio, a at home, to the house
dominare dominate
donna woman
dopodomani the day after
 tomorrow
doppio *m.* double
dopo, dopo di after
dormire to sleep
dotto learned
dottore *m.* doctor

dove where
dov'è? where is?
dovere must, to have to, owe
dovere *m.* duty
dovunque anywhere, everywhere
dovuto due
dozzina dozen
dubbio doubt
due two
dunque therefore
durante during
durare to last
duraturo lasting
duro tough, hard

E

e, ed and
ebreo Jewish
eccellente excellent
eccetto except
ecco here is, here are; there is,
 there are
economico economical
edificio building
Egitto Egypt
egli he
eguale equal, even, alike
elegante elegant, stylish
elettricità electricity
elettrico electric
ella she
entusiasmo enthusiasm
entusiasta *m. & f.* enthusiastic
entrare to enter, come in
epoca epoch, era
eppure yet, nevertheless
eruzione *f.* eruption
esagerare exaggerate
esaminare to examine
esattamente exactly
esattezza exactness
esatto exact
esempio example
esistere exist
esplorare to explore
esportare to export
espressione *f.* expression
essa *f.* she, it
esse *f.* they, them
essenziale essential
essi *m.* they, them
estasiato ecstatic

estate *f.* summer
estero foreign
    ..., all' abroad
estivo *adj.* summer
età age (of a person)
eterno eternal
evento event
evitare to avoid

F

fabbrica factory
fabbricazione *f.* manufacture
faccia face
facile easy
fame *f.* hunger
    avere ... to be hungry
famiglia family
famoso famous
fango mud
    c'è ... it's muddy
fare to do, to make
    ... colazione to have breakfast
farmacia drugstore, pharmacy
fascino charm
favorevole favorable
favorisca! come in!
fazzoletto handkerchief
febbraio February
febbre *f.* fever
fedele faithful
felice happy
felicità happiness
feltro felt
fermare to stop
fermato stopped
ferrovia railroad
fervente burning, fervent
festa festival, holiday
fiamma flame
fianco (*pl.* fianchi) hip
fico (*pl.* fichi) fig
fidanzato fiance
figlia daughter
figlio son
figuri, sì! of course! you can
    imagine!
fila row, line
    in ... on line
filetto filet, filet mignon
film *m.* film, motion picture
filo thread

finalmente finally
finestra window
finire to finish
fino a up to, until, as far as
fiore *m.* flower
firmare to sign
fisico physicist
fiume *m.* river
flanella flannel
folla crowd
fontana fountain
fonografo phonograph
forbici *f. pl.* scissors
forchetta fork
forestiero foreigner
formaggio cheese
formalità formality
formato format, shape
forse maybe, perhaps
forte loud, strong
fortuna luck
    per ... luckily
fortunato fortunate, lucky
fotografia photograph
    fare una ... to take a picture
fra between, among
francese *m. & f.* French
Francia France
fratello brother
frattempo, nel in the meantime
freddo cold
    fa ... it is cold
frequentemente frequently
fresco *adj.* fresh, cool
    fa ... it is cool
fretta hurry
    ho ... I am in a hurry
friggere to fry
frigorifero refrigerator
frittata omelet
fritto fried
frutta fruit (at the table)
frutto fruit
fumare to smoke
funicolare *f.* funicular, cable railway
funziona, non it is out of order

G

gabbia cage
gabinetto toilet
galante gallant

galanteria gallantry
galosce f. pl. overshoes, rubbers
gamba leg
gas m. gas
gatto cat
gelato ice cream
gelo frost
   si gela it's freezing
geloso jealous
generalmente ordinarily, generally,
   usually
genio genius
genitore m. parent
gennaio January
gentile kind
gentilezza kindness
geologo geologist
ghiaccio ice
già already
giacca jacket, coat
   ... lenta loose jacket
   ... aderente close fitting jacket
giacchè inasmuch as, since
giallo yellow
giardino garden
gigantesco gigantic
giocare to play
giocatore m. player
giocattolo toy
giogo yoke
gioia joy
giornale m. newspaper, journal
   (business)
giornata day (in its duration)
giorno day
giovane young
giovedì m. Thursday
gita trip
giugno June
giustizia justice
   palazzo di ... court house
gloria glory
golfo gulf
gomma rubber, eraser
gonnella skirt
governare to govern, rule
gradevole agreeable
grado degree
grande big, large
grano wheat
grasso fat

grato grateful
gratis free
grave serious, grave
gravità gravity
grazie thank you
grazioso pretty
Grecia Greece
gridare to shout, cry
grido scream
grigio gray
grillo cricket
gruppo group
guadagno profit, gain
guanto glove
guarnizioni f. pl. trimmings
guasto n. damage, something out
   of order
guerra war
guida guide
guidare drive
gusto taste

H

ha you (pol. sing.) have, he has,
   she has
hai you (fam. sing.) have
hanno you (polite pl.) have, they
   have
ho I have

I

idea idea
ideare to conceive
immensamente immensely
incantevole enchanting
incontrare to meet
incontro meeting
indossare wear
indubbiamente undoubtedly
ieri yesterday
ignorante ignorant
ignoranza ignorance
illustrazione f. illustration
illustre illustrious
imbarcarsi to embark, sail
immaginare to imagine
immediatamente immediately,
   at once
immortale immortal
imparare to learn

impermeabile m. raincoat
Impero Romano Roman Empire
impiegato employed; n. employee
imponente imposing
importa, non it doesn't matter
importare to import; to be of
    consequence
impossibile impossible
impossibilità impossibility
impressione f. impression
in in
incantevole enchanting
inchiostro ink
inciso engraved
includere include
indescrivibilmente indescribably
indicare to indicate, point
indietro behind
    va ... it is slow (of a watch)
indimenticabile unforgettable
indirizzo address, direction
indovinare to guess
indubbiamente undoubtedly
industria industry
industriale industrial
inestimabile incalculable
infanzia childhood
infatti in fact
infinito infinite
informare inform
ingegnere m. engineer
Inghilterra England
inglese m. & f. English
ingrosso, all' wholesale
iniziare to start
innegabile undeniable
insalata salad
insegnare to teach
insieme together
insipido tasteless
intanto meanwhile
intellettuale intellectual
intelligente intelligent
intende, s'- of course, it's understood
interessante interesting
intero entire
interrogazione f. question
interrompere interrupt
intimo intimate
intrepido intrepid, fearless
intrusione f. intrusion
inutile useless

invano in vain
introduzione f. introduction
invaso taken hold, invaded
invasore m. invader
invece instead
inventore m. inventor
inverno winter
invitare to invite
invitato guest
invocante invoking
io I
isola island
isoletta small island
ispirazione f. inspiration
Italia Italy
italiano Italian
itinerario itinerary

L

là there
labirinto labyrinth
laborioso hard working
laggiù down there
lagnarsi to complain
lago lake
lagrima tear
laguna lagoon
lametta razor blade
lampada lamp
lampadina lamp bulb
lampo lighting
lampeggia it's lighting
lana wool
lancetta hand (of a watch or clock)
lanciare to throw
lapis m. pencil
largo wide, large
lasciare to leave, to let, allow
lassù up there
lato side
latte m. milk
lattuga lettuce
lava lava
lavabo wash basin
lavanderia laundry
lavarsi to wash oneself
legale legal
legalizzare legalize
legge f. law
legno wood
legumi m. pl. vegetables, legumes

lei you *(pol. sing.)*
lento slow
lenzuolo *(pl.* **le lenzuola)** bed sheet
leone *m.* lion
lettera letter
   ... di cambio letter of exchange
letteratura literature
letto bed
lezione *f.* lesson
lì there
liberazione *f.* liberation
libero free, unoccupied
libro book
   ... di cassa cash book
   ... mastro ledger
lido seashore
lieto glad
limone *m.* lemon
lingua language, tongue
lino linen
liscio smooth
   non se la passa liscia you won't
   get away with it
lista list
   ... delle vivande menu
   ... dei vini wine list
logico logical
Londra London
lontano far
loro you *(pol. pl.),* they, them
luce *f.* light
   ... elettrica electric light
luglio July
luminoso bright
luna moon
   ... di miele honeymoon
lunedì *m.* Monday
lungo long
   a ... for a long time
luogo *(pl.* **luoghi)** place
lupo wolf
lusso luxury
lussureggiante luxurious,
   luxuriant

M

ma but, however
macchina machine, car
   ... cinematografica movie camera
   ... da cucire sewing machine

   ... da scrivere typewriter
   ... fotografica camera
madre *f.* mother
maestro teacher
maggio May
maggiore major
   la maggior parte most, the
   majority
magnifico magnificent, wonderful
mai never
   non ... (verb) **... mai** never
maiale *m.* pork
mal di testa headache
malamente badly
malato ill
male bad
   non c'è ... not bad
   sto ... I am ill, I feel sick
mamma mother
mancia tip
mangiare to eat
manica *(pl.* **maniche)** sleeve
mantenere to keep
marciapiede *m.* sidewalk
mare *m.* sea
marina navy
marito husband
marmellata jam
marmo marble
martedì *m.* Tuesday
martello hammer
marzo March
massimo maximum
matematico mathematician
materasso mattress
matita pencil
mattina morning
   di or la ... in the morning
mattino morning
me me
meccanismo movement (of a watch)
medicina medicine
medico doctor, physician
medioevale medieval
medio evo Middle Ages
meglio better
mela apple
melodioso melodious
meno less
   a ... che unless

mensilmente monthly
mente *f.* mind
mentire to lie
mentre while
meraviglia marvel, wonder
meravigliosamente marvelously
meraviglioso wonderful, marvelous
mercato market
  a buon . . . cheap, inexpensive
merce *f.* merchandise
mercoledì Wednesday
meritare to deserve
merletto lace
mese *m.* month
messa Mass
messaggio message
metà half
mettere to put, put on
metro meter
mezzanotte *f.* midnight
mezzo middle, half, means
  non c'è altra via di . . . there is no
  other way
mezzogiorno noon
miei *m. pl.* my, mine
microscopio microscope
miei my, mine
miele *m.* honey
migliaïa *f. pl.* thousands
migliorare to get better
migliore better
mila (*pl.* mille) one thousand
milione *m.* million
milite *m.* soldier
  Milite Ignoto Unknown Soldier
minacciare to threaten
minestrone *m.* minestrone, thick
  vegetable soup
minuto minute
minuto, al retail
mio my, mine
mischiare mix
misura measurement, measure, size
  prendere la . . . to take the
  measurement
mite mild
mobile *adj.* movable; *n. m.* piece of
  furniture
mobilia furniture

modello pattern, model
moderato moderate, reasonable
moda fashion
moderazione *f.* moderation
moderno modern
modesto modest
modo manner
  in ispecial . . . especially
mogano mahogany
moglie *f.* wife
molla spring
molo pier
moltissimo very much
molto *adj.* much, a great deal;
  adv. very
momento moment
  . . ., al at present
mondiale of the world
mondo world
montagna mountain
monumento monument
moro Moor
morso bite
mostrare to show
motocicletta motorcycle
motore *m.* motor
municipio city hall
muovere move
muro wall
museo museum
musica music
musicista *m. & f.* musician
mutande *f. pl.* underwear, shorts

N

nacque was born
nascere to be born
nascita birth
napoletano Neapolitan
nastro ribbon
naturalmente naturally
Natale *m.* Christmas
naturale natural
naturalmente naturally
nazione *f.* nation
nazionalità *f.* nationality
nè . . . nè neither . . . nor

nebbia fog
  c'è ... it's foggy
necessità necessity
negare to deny
negozio store
nemico (*pl.* nemici) enemy
nemmeno not even
nero black
nessuno nobody
neve *f.* snow
nevica it is snowing
niente nothing
  ... affatto not at all
nipote *m.* nephew; *f.* niece
no no
nobile *m.n.* nobleman; *adj.* noble
noce nut (tree *m.*; fruit *f.*)
  ... di cocco cocoanut
noi we
noleggio, prendere in to rent
nome *m.* name
nonna grandmother
nonno grandfather
nono ninth
nord *m.* north
normalmente usually, normally
nostalgia nostalgia, longing
nota note
notare to note, notice
notaio notary
notte *f.* night
novanta ninety
nove nine
novella short story
novembre *m.* November
nulla nothing
numero number, size
nuotare to swim
nuovamente again
nuovo new
nutriente nutritious
nuvola cloud
nuvoloso cloudy

O

o or
occasione *f.* occasion
  colgo questa ... I take this
  occasion

occupare occupy
occupato busy, occupied
odiare to hate
odorare to smell
offerta *n.* offer
offrire to offer
oggetto object
oggi today
  al giorno d'... nowadays
  ... ad otto a week from today
  ... stesso this very day
ogni each, every
ognuno everyone, everybody
Olanda Holland
olio oil
oliva olive
olivo olive tree
oltre more, beside
ombra shade, shadow
ombrello umbrella
onda wave
onesto honest
onorario fee
onore *m.* honor
  fare ... to honor
opera opera, work
  ... d'arte work of art
opinione *f.* opinion
oppure or, otherwise
opuscolo pamphlet
ora *n.* hour, time
  che ... è? what time is it?
ora *adv.* now
  da ... in poi from now on
  proprio ... just now
  fin da ... as of now
orario timetable
  in ... on time
orecchio ear
orgoglio pride
orgoglioso proud
origine *f.* origin
orlo edge
ormai (oramai) by now
oro gold
orologeria watchmaker's shop
orologiaio watchmaker

orologio watch
    ... a pendolo wall clock
    ... a sveglia alarm clock
    ... da polso wrist watch
    ... da tasca pocket watch
orrendo horrendous, horrible
oscillazione f. oscillation, swinging
oscurità darkness
ospedale m. hospital
ospitale hospitable
ospitalità hospitality
ospite m. & f. guest
ottanta eighty
ottavo eighth
ottimo excellent
otto eight
ottobre m. October
ovest west
ovunque anywhere, everywhere

P

pacco package
pacchetto little package
pace f. peace
padre m. father
paese m. country
Paesi Bassi Netherlands
pagamento payment
pagare to pay
paio pair
palazzo building, palace
palma palm tree, palm
panciera girdle
panciotto vest
pane m. bread
panino roll (bread)
panorama m. panorama, view
pantofola slipper
Papa m. Pope
paradiso paradise
paralume m. lamp shade
parapioggia m. umbrella
parata parade
parco (pl. **parchi**) park
parente m. & f. relative
pari even
Parigi Paris
parlare to speak
parola word
parte f. part

la maggior ... the larger part, most
    da questa ... this way
partenza departure
partire to leave, to depart
partita n. game, contest
Pasqua Easter
passaporto passport
passare to pass, to spend (time)
passatempo pastime
passeggiata walk
passeggio n. walk, walking
    da ... for walking
pasticcino pastry
pasto meal
patata potato
    purè di patate mashed potatoes
patria homeland, mother country
patriottico patriotic
paura fear
    ho ... I am afraid
pecora sheep
pedone m. pedestrian
peggio worse
pelle f. leather, skin
pellicola film, motion picture
pena pain
    non vale la ... it is not worthwhile
pendolo pendulum
penicillina penicillin
penna pen
    ... stilografica fountain pen
pensare to think
pensatore f. thinker
pensiero thought
pensione f. board, boarding house
pentirsi to repent, regret
pepe m. pepper
per for
per cento per cent
perchè because
perchè? why?
perdere to lose
perdonare to forgive, pardon
peregrinazione f. wandering
perenne perennial, everlasting
perfettamente perfectly
perfetto perfect
perfezione f. perfection
pericolo danger
pericoloso dangerous
periferia suburbs

periodo period
permanenza stay
permettere to permit, allow
però however
persona person
personale personal
pesante heavy
pesare to weigh
pesarsi to weigh oneself
pesca, la fishing
pescare to fish
pesce *m.* fish
peso weight
petrolio petroleum
pettine *m.* comb
pezzo piece
piacere to like; *n.m.* pleasure, favor
    per . . . please
piacevole pleasant, agreeable
piangere to cry, weep
piano floor, story (of a house)
pianura plain
pianta map, plant
pianterreno ground floor
piatto dish, plate
piattino saucer
piazza square
piccante sharp, spicy
piccolo small
piede *f.* foot
piacevole agreeable
pietanza course (of a dinner)
pigliare to catch
pigione *f.* rent
pillola pill
pioggia rain
piove it is raining
piroscafo ship, steamer, liner
pittore *m.* painter
pittoresco picturesque
più more
pitturare to paint
po', un a little, some
pochino a very little bit
poco (*pl.* pochi) little, some
    . . . fa a while ago
poesia poem
poi after, then
poichè since, inasmuch as

politico political
polizia police
polizza di carico bill of lading
pollo chicken
    . . . arrosto roast chicken
    . . . alla cacciatora chicken fricassee
Polonia Poland
polsino cuff (of a shirt)
polso pulse, wrist
poltrona armchair
pomeriggio afternoon
pomodoro tomato
    salsa di pomodori tomato sauce
pompelmo grapefruit
ponte *m.* bridge
popolare popular
popolo people
porgere to give, to hand
porta door
portamonete *m.* change purse
portare to carry, to bring
porto port
possibile possible
posso I can
posta post office, mail
    . . . aerea air mail
posto place
potente powerful
potere to be able to
povero poor
pranzare to dine
pranzo dinner
    a . . . at dinner, for dinner
precisamente precisely, exactly
preciso precise; sharp (of hours)
prediletto cherished
preferenza preference
preferire to prefer
pregare to pray, beg
prego don't mention it (in reply to
    grazie)
prendere to take
prenotare to reserve
prenotazione *f.* reservation
preoccupazione *f.* worry
preparare to prepare
prepararsi to get ready
presentare to introduce, present
presente present

presenza presence
press'a poco just about
prestare to lend
presto soon, early
  a . . . see you soon
prezioso precious
prezzo price
prigioniero prisoner
prima before
  . . . di tutto before everything else
primavera spring
primo first
principe *m.* prince
probabilmente probably
procedere to proceed
procura power of attorney
prodotto product
professore *m.* professor
profondità depth
profumeria perfume shop
profumo perfume
programma *m.* program
prolungare prolong
promessa promise
pronto ready
pronunzia pronounciation
proposito, a by the way
propriamente exactly
proprio own, real, really
prosatore *m.* prose writer
prosciutto Italian ham
prossimo next
protesta protest
provare to try, try on
pubblico public
pulire to clean
punto point; period; stitch
puntuale punctual
può can
  si . . . may I come in?
purtroppo unfortunately

Q

quaderno notebook
quadrante *m.* face (of a watch)
quadro picture
qualche cosa something
quale? which?
qualcuno somebody
qualità quality

qualora whenever
qualsiasi any, no matter which
qualunque any
quando when
quanto as, as much, how much?
  a . . . mi è stato detto from what I
  have been told
quaranta forty
quartiere *m.* quarter (of a city)
quarto fourth, quarter
quasi nearly, almost
quattordici fourteen
quattro four
questo this
qui here
quindi therefore
quindici fifteen
quindicina about fifteen, a fortnight
quinto fifth
quotidiano daily

R

raccolta collection
rada bay, road
radio *f.* radio
radunarsi to go together
raffreddore *m.* cold
  prendere un . . . to catch a cold
ragazza girl
ragazzino little boy
ragazzo boy
raggiungere to reach
ragione *f.* reason
  avere . . . to be right
rammentare to remind
ramo branch (of a tree)
rapido rapid
rappresaglia reprisal
rappresentante *m.* representative,
  agent
rappresentazione *f.* performance
raro rare
rasoio razor
rata rate
re *m.* king
recente recent
recentemente recently
redigere to draw up
reggipetto brassiere
regina queen

regione *f.* region
registro register
regno kingdom
religione *f.* religion
religioso religious
reliquia relic
repubblica republic
repentino sudden
residenziale residential
restaurato restored
resto remainder, change, rest
restrizione *f.* restriction
ricamo embroidery
ricchezza wealth
ricco *(m.pl.* ricchi; *f.pl.* ricche) rich
ricetta prescription
ricevere to receive
ricevuta receipt ·
riconoscente grateful
riconoscere recognize
ricordare to remember; to record
ricordarsi to remember
ricordo souvenir
ridere to laugh
riempire to fill
rifiutare to refuse
rifugiarsi to seek refuge
riga ruler
rimanere to remain
Rinascimento Renaissance
ringraziare to thank
riparare to repair, fix
ripetere to repeat
riposarsi to rest
riposo rest
riscaldamento heat
    ... centrale central heating
riscuotere to cash
riso laughter, rice
risorto resurrected
risparmiare to save
rispondere to answer
ristorante *m.* restaurant
risurrezione resurrection
ritornare to return
riunirsi to gather, to meet
rivedere to see again
rivelare reveal
rivincita return match
roccioso rocky
romanzo novel
rompere to break, tear

rosa rose
rosso red
rotto broken
rovinato ruined, damaged
rubare to rob, steal
rubino ruby, jewel (of a watch)
ruderi *m.pl.* ruins
rullo roll
Rumenia or Romania Rumania
ruota wheel
Russia Russia
russo Russian

S

sabato Saturday
sacrificio sacrifice
sala room, hall
    ... da pranzo dining room
    ... d'aspetto waiting room
salato salted, salty
sale *m.* salt
salire to go up, climb
salotto living room
salsa sauce
saltare to jump
salutare to greet
saluto greeting
salute *f.* health
San Giovanni St. John
sangue *m.* blood
    al ... rare (meat)
sanguinoso bloody
San Paolo St. Paul
San Pietro St. Peter
Santa Maria St. Mary
Santa Sede *f.* Holy See
santo *adj.* holy, saintly; *n.* saint
santuario sanctuary
sapere to know
sapone *m.* soap
sarta dressmaker
sarto tailor
sartoria tailor shop
sasso stone
sbagliarsi to be mistaken
sbaglio mistake, error
    se non mi ... if I am not mistaken
sbalzato embossed
sbrigare to settle, regulate
sbrigarsi to get through
sbrighiamoci let's hurry

scacchi *m. pl.* chess
scala stairway, ladder
scale stairs
scambio exchange
scarpa shoe
scatola box
scavi *m. pl.* excavations
scegliere to choose
scelto chosen
scena scene
scendere to descend
scherzare to joke, jest
scienza science
scienziato scientist
scivolare to slip, glide
scolpito sculptured
scommettere to bet, wager
scompartimento compartment
scoprire to discover
scoraggiato discouraged
scorretto incorrect
scritto written
scrittoio desk
scrittore *m.* writer
scrivere to write
  ... a macchina to typewrite
scultore *m.* sculptor
scuola school
scusare to excuse
  scusi! excuse me!
se if
sebbene although
secco dry
secolo century
secondo second; according to
sedano celery
sede *f.* office
  ... centrale main office
sedersi to sit
sedia chair
sedici sixteen
sedile *m.* seat
segno sign
segretamente secretly
seguire to follow
sei six
sembrare to seem
  mi sembra it seems to me
semplice simple
semplicemente simply, just
sempre always

sentire feel, hear
senza without
senz'altro without fail
sepolto buried
sera evening
serata evening (in its duration)
servire to serve
servirla, al at your service
sessanta sixty
sesto sixth
seta silk
sete *f.* thirst
  avere ... to be thirsty
settanta seventy
sette seven
settembre *m.* September
settimana week
  ... prossima next week
  ... scorsa last week
settimo seventh
sfuggire escape
sfuggita, di hastily
si one, people, they
  ... dice they say
sì yes
siccome since, inasmuch as
sicuro sure, certain
  di ... for sure
sigaretta cigarette
sigaro cigar
significato meaning
signor mister
signora Mrs., madam, lady, wife
signore sir, gentleman
signorina miss, young lady
silenzio silence
silenziosamente silently
simile similar
simpatico charming, nice
sindaco mayor
sinistra, a to the left
sintomo symptom
sistemarsi to get settled
sito situated, located
soffocante suffocating, stifling
sognare to dream
sogno dream
sole *m.* sun
  il ... brilla the sun is shining
  il ... tramonta the sun is setting

solito usual
    più del . . . more than usual
solo *adv.* only; *adj.* alone, only,
    single
soltanto only
sono, ci there are
sontuoso sumptuous
sopra on, over
soprabito overcoat
soprascarpe *f.pl.* overshoes, rubbers
sorella sister
sorgere to rise
sostituire to replace
sottana slip, petticoat
sottile thin
sotto beneath, under
sottomarino submarine
spaghetti *m. pl.* spaghetti
Spagna Spain
spagnuolo Spanish, Spaniard
spalancare to open wide
spalla shoulder
sparire to disappear
spaventarsi to get frightened
spazzola brush
spazzolare to brush
spazzolino tooth brush
specchio mirror
speciale special
specialmente especially
spedire to send
spedizione *m.* expedition
spegnere to extinguish
sperare to hope
spesso often
spettacolo spectacle
spiaggia beach
spiccioli *m. pl.* change (money)
spiegare to explain, unfold
spiegarsi to make oneself clear
spinaci *m. pl.* spinach
spinto driven, pushed
splendore *m.* splendor
sporco dirty
sportello window, pay window
    (of a bank)
sposa bride, wife
sposare to marry
sposina dear little wife
sposini newlyweds
sprecare to waste
spugna sponge

squadra team
squillare ring out
squisito delicious, exquisite
stabile *m.* building, house
stabilire to establish
stagione *f.* season
stagno tin
stanco tired
stare to stay
    . . . a pennello to fit perfectly
    . . . in piedi to stand up
    . . . per to be about to
stasera tonight
Stati Uniti *m. pl.* United States
stato state
statua statue
stazione *f.* station
    . . . balneare *f.* bathing resort
sterlina pound sterling
sternutire to sneeze
stesso same
stile *m.* style
stizzito angry
stoffa material, cloth
stomaco stomach
storia history, story
storico historical
strada street, road
strage *f.* slaughter
strano strange
stretto tight, narrow
studente *m.* student
studio study
stufa stove
stupendo stupendous
stupido stupid
sua *f.* his, her, hers, your, yours
subito at once; quickly
sublime sublime
successore *m.* successor
succursale *f.* branch (of a firm)
sud *m.* south
sudare to perspire
sudore *m.* perspiration
sigillo seal
suo his, her, hers, your, yours
suoi *pl.* his, her, hers, your, yours
suola sole (of a shoe)
suonare to ring; strike (the hour);
    to play (an instrument)
superfluo superfluous
supporre to suppose

svegliarsi to wake up
svestirsi to undress
sviluppo development
svizzero Swiss

T

tabacco tobacco
tacco (*pl.* tacchi) heel
tanti, tante many
tanto so, so much
tappeto rug
tardi late
  più . . . later
tasca pocket
tassa tax, duty
tassì *m.* taxi
tavola table
tazza cup
tè *m.* tea
teatro theater
tedesco (*pl.* tedeschi) German
telefonare to telephone
telefono telephone
telegramma *m.* telegram
telegrafare to telegraph
telescopio telescope
televisione *f.* television
temperatura temperature
tempesta storm
tempo time, weather
  in or a . . . on time
  fa bel . . . the weather is fine
  . . . disponibile free time
tendina curtain
tenere to hold, keep
  . . . il resto to keep the change
tenero tender
termometro thermometer
terra earth
terribile terrible
terzo third
tesoro treasure
tessuto cloth, fabric
testa head
testimonio witness
titolo title, security
toccare to touch
  ci toccherà we shall have to
togliere to take away from
toletta dressing table

tomba tomb
Torre Pendente *f.* Leaning Tower
torrenti, a pouring
torta cake
totale *n.m. & adj.* total
tovaglia tablecloth
tovagliolo napkin
tra between, among
tracciare trace, outline
tracciato outlined
tradurre to translate
traffico traffic
tramonto sunset
transazione *f.* transaction
trasportare to transport
trasporto transportation
tratta draft
trattenersi to remain
tre three
tredici thirteen
treno train
trenta thirty
tromba horn (of a car)
troppo too, too much
trovare to find
trovarsi to be; to be located; to find
  oneself
trucidato slaughtered
truppe *f. pl.* troops
tu you (*fam. sing.*)
tuono thunder
  tuona it is thundering
Turchia Turkey
turista *m.* tourist
tutt'altro! on the contrary, anything
  but!
tuttavia nevertheless
tutto all, everything

U

uccello bird
udienza audience
udire to hear
ufficio office
  . . . postale post office
uguale alike, equal
ultimo last
umidità humidity, dampness
umido humid, damp
umile humble

undici eleven
unito united
università university
uno one
uomo (*pl.* **gli uomini**) man
uovo (*pl.* **le uova**) egg
uragano hurricane
urgente urgent
usanza custom
usare to use, employ
uscita exit
uso use, usage
utile useful
uva grape

V

va bene all right
vacanza vacation
valido valid
valigia (*pl.* **valigie**) valise, suitcase
valore *m.* value, security
vano room (empty, unfurnished)
vapore *m.* steamboat
varietà variety
vasca washtub
vasellame *m.* china
vasto large, vest
Vaticano Vatican
vecchio old
vedere to see
veduta view
veicolo vehicle
velluto velvet
veloce fast
vendere to sell
venerdì Friday
venire to come
venti twenty
ventina about twenty
vento wind
   tira . . . it is windy
venturo next
venuta *n.* coming
veramente really, truly
verde green

verdura green vegetables
verità truth
vero true, real
vertigini *f. pl.* dizziness
   avere le . . . to be dizzy
veste *f.* dress
vestiario clothing
vestirsi to dress (oneself)
vestito suit
   confezionare un . . . to make a suit
vetro glass, crystal
vettura car (of a train); carriage
via *n.* street, avenue; *adv.* away
   per . . . aerea by the mail
viaggiare to travel
viaggiatore *m.* traveler
viaggio trip, voyage
   . . . di nozze honeymoon trip
vicino near; *n.* neighbor
vigilia eve
vino wine
visibile visible
visita visit
visitare to visit
vita waistline, life
vitella veal
vittoria victory
vocabolario vocabulary
voce *f.* voice
voi you (*fam. pl.*)
volentieri willingly
volere to want, wish
volta turn; way; road
   una . . . once
   qualche . . . sometimes
   delle volte at times
voltare turn over
vulcano volcano
vuoto empty

Z

zero zero
zia aunt
zio uncle
zonzo, andare a to wander about
zuccheriera sugar bowl
zucchero sugar

English-Italian
Dictionary

a, an uno, una, un
able, to be potere, essere capace
about circa
above sopra, al disopra
abroad all'estero
absolutely assolutamente
accept, to accettare
accident accidente
accompany, to accompagnare
according, to secondo
accustomed abituato
ache dolore
acquaintance conoscenza
action azione
add, to aggiungere
address indirizzo
admire, to ammirare
advance, in in anticipo
advice consiglio
advise, to consigliare
afraid, I am ho paura
after dopo, poi
afternoon pomeriggio
again nuovamente
against contro
age età (of a person)
agency agenzia
agent agente m., rappresentante m.
agreeable gradevole, piacevole
agriculture agricoltura
ahead avanti
air aria
air mail posta aerea
airplane aeroplano
airport aeroporto
alarm, to allarmare

alike uguale, eguale, simile
all tutto, tutti, tutte
allow, to permettere
all right va bene
almost quasi
alone solo
already già
also anche, pure
although benchè, sebbene
always sempre
American americano
among fra, tra
amount ammontare n. (m.) & v.
amusement divertimento
amusing divertente
ancient antico
and e, ed
angry adirato, stizzito, arrabbiato,
   in collera
animal animale m.
announce, to annunziare
answer, to rispondere
answer riscontro, risposta
anxious ansioso
any alcuno
anyone chiunque, ognuno
anywhere dovunque, ovunque
apartment appartamento
appear, to apparire
appetite appetito
appetizer antipasto
apple mela
appointment appuntamento
appreciate, appreziare
approach, to avvicinarsi
approve, to approvare
April aprile m.
arm braccio (pl. le braccia)

armchair poltrona
arrival arrivo
arrive, to arrivare
art arte *f.*
article articolo
artist artista *m. & f.*
as come
ask, to chiedere, domandare
asleep, to fall addormentarsi
assure, to assicurare, accertare
at a
at all affatto
at once subito
attend, to assistere
attraction attrazione *f.*
attractive attraente
August agosto
aunt zia
authentic autentico
author autore *m.*
authority autorità
automobile automobile *f.*
autumn autunno
avenue via
aviation aviazione *f.*
avoid, to evitare
away via
awaken, to svegliarsi

B

bad cattivo *m.*
  not ... non c'è male
badly malamente
baggage bagaglio
bank banca
basket cesta, paniere
bath bagno
bathe, to fare il bagno
bathroom bagno, stanza da bagno
bathtub vasca
battle battaglia
be, to essere, trovarsi, stare
beach spiaggia
beat battere
beautiful bel, bella, bello
beauty bellezza
because perchè
become, to diventare
bed letto
bedroom camera da letto
bed sheet lenzuolo (*pl.* le lenzuola)

beef bue *m.*
before prima
begin, to cominciare, incominciare
behind dietro, indietro
Belgium Belgio
believe, to credere
bell campanello
below sotto, al disotto
belt cintura
beneath sotto
beside accanto, oltre
bet, to scommettere
better migliore *adj.;* meglio *adv.*
  to get ... migliorare
between tra, fra
bicycle bicicletta
big grande
bill conto
bird uccello
birth nascita
bite morso
bitter amaro
black nero
blanket coperta
bless, to benedire
blond biondo
blood sangue *m.*
blouse camicetta
blue azzurro, celeste
boarding house pensione *f.*
boat barca
body corpo
boil, to bollire
book libro
born, to be nascere
both ambedue, tutti e due
bottle bottiglia
box scatola
boy ragazzo, fanciullo
brassiere reggipetto
Brazil Brasile *m.*
bread pane *m.*
break, to rompere
breakfast colazione *f.*
  to have ... fare colazione
bride sposa
bridge ponte *m.*
brief breve
bright luminoso
brilliant brillante
bring, to portare
broad largo

brother fratello
brother-in-law cognato
brown bruno,-a, marrone
brunette brunetta
brush spazzola
brush, to spazzolare
build, to costruire
building palazzo, edificio, stabile m.
to burn ardere, bruciare
bus autobus
business affari
   to do . . . fare affari
busy occupato
but ma, però
butcher shop macelleria
butter burro
button bottone m.
buy, to comprare
by per
by means of mediante, per mezzo di
by chance per caso

C

cabin cabina
cake torta
calendar calendario
call, to chiamare
called, to be (name) chiamarsi
camera macchina fotografica
Canada Canadà m.
cap berretto
captain capitano
car (railroad) carrozza, vagone
   (automobile) macchina,
   automobile
card biglietto visita,
   carta da gioco
career carriera
carry, to portare, trasportare
cash, to riscuotere
cashier cassiere
cat gatto
catch, to pigliare, prendere
cathedral cattedrale f.
catholic cattolico, cattolici m.pl.,
   cattoliche f.pl.
celebrate, to celebrare
cemetery cimitero
cent centesimo, soldo

center centro
centigrade centigrado
central centrale
century secolo
cereal cereale
certain certo, sicuro
certainly certamente
chair sedia
change (money) spiccioli m. pl.
charm fascino
charming simpatico
chauffeur autista m.
cheap a buon mercato
check (bill) conto
   (money) assegno
check room (for baggage) deposito
   (di) bagagli
cheerfully allegramente
cheese formaggio
chestnut castagna
chicken pollo
child bambino,-a
childhood infanzia
chocolate cioccolata
choose, to scegliere
Christmas Natale m.
church chiesa
cigar sigaro
cigarette sigaretta
city città
city hall municipio
civilization civiltà
class classe f.
clean to, pulire
climate clima m.
climb salire
close, to chiudere
closet armadio
cloth tessuto, stoffa
clothing vestiario
cloud nuvola
cloudy nuvoloso
coal carbone m.
coast costa
coat giacca
coffee caffè m.
collapse, to crollare
cold freddo n. & adj.
   (illness) raffreddore m.
collar colletto

collection raccolta
color colore *m.*
comb pettine *m.*
come, to venire
come in, to entrare
come in! favorisca!
comfort conforto
comfortable comodo
  to make oneself ... accomodarsi
commerce commercio
commercial commerciale
company compagnia
complain, to lagnarsi
complete completo
completely completamente
concert concerto
condition condizione *f.*
confess, to confessare
consist of, to consistere di
construct, to costruire
contrary contrario, opposto
  on the ... al contrario
conversation conversazione *f.*
convince, to convincere
cook, to cucinare, cuocere
cooked cotto
cool fresco
copy copia
corner angolo
correspondence corrispondenza
cost, to costare
cotton cotone *m.*
count, to contare
country paese *m.,* campagna
couple paio, coppia
courage coraggio
course (of a dinner) pietanza
course, of si figuri, beninteso,
  s'intende
courtesy cortesia
cousin cugino,-a
cover, to coprire
cream crema
credit credito
cry, to gridare (shout), piangere
  (weep)
cuff (of a shirt) polsino
cup tazza
curtain tendina
custom usanza, costume *m.*

customs dogana
  ... inspection controllo della
  dogana
  ... officer doganiere *m.*
cut, to tagliare
Czechoslovakia Ceco-slovacchia

D

daily quotidiano
damage guasto
damp umido
dance ballo
  to ... ballare
danger pericolo
dangerous pericoloso
dark scuro, buio
darkness oscurità
date appuntamento, data, dattero
daughter figlia
dawn alba
day giorno, giornata
dear caro
December dicembre *m.*
decide, to decidere
decision decisione
declare, to dichiarare
deep cupo, profondo
degree grado
delicious delizioso, squisito
deliver, to consegnare
demand, to domandare
dentist dentista *m. & f.*
deny, to negare
depart, to partire
departure partenza
deposit, to depositare
descend, to scendere, andar giù
describe, to descrivere
description descrizione *f.*
deserve, to meritare
desire, to desiderare
desk scrittoio, scrivania
dessert dolce *m.*
diamond diamante *m.*
dictionary dizionario
difference differenza
different differente, diverso
difficult difficile
difficulty difficoltà
dine, to pranzare

dining room sala da pranzo
dinner pranzo
direction indirizzo, direzione *f.*
directly direttamente
dirty sporco, sudicio
disappear, to sparire
discover, to scoprire
discuss, to discutere
dish piatto
distance distanza
distant distante
disturb, to disturbare
divide, to dividere
do, to fare
doctor dottore *m.*, medico
dog cane *m.*
dollar dollaro
donkey asino
door porta
doorbell campanello
double doppio
doubt dubbio
   to ... dubitare
dozen dozzina
draft corrente d'aria; (commercial) tratta
dream sogno
dream, to sognare
dress veste *f.*
dressmaker sarta
dress (oneself), to vestirsi
drink, to bere
drive, to guidare
driver autista *m.*
drugstore farmacia
dry secco
during durante
dwell abitare

E

each ogni
eager ansioso
ear orecchio
early di buon'ora, presto
earth terra
Easter Pasqua
easy facile
eat, to mangiare
egg uovo, *pl.* le uova
eight otto

eighteen diciotto
eighty ottanta
electric elettrico
electricity elettricità
elegant elegante
elevator ascensore *m.*
eleven undici
embark, to imbarcarsi
embrace, to abbracciare
embroidery ricamo
empty vuoto
enchanting incantevole
enemy nemico, nemici *pl.*
engineer ingegnere *m.*
England Inghilterra
English Inglese *m.&f.*
enough abbastanza
enter, to entrare
enthusiasm entusiamo
enthusiastic entusiasta
entire intero
envelope busta
epoch epoca
equal eguale
error sbaglio, errore *m.*
escape, to fuggire, scappare
especially in ispecial modo, specialmente
essential essenziale
establish, to stabilire
eternal eterno
even pari
evening sera, serata
event evento
every ogni
everyone ognuno
everything tutto
everywhere dappertutto, dovunque, ovunque
exact esatto
exactly propriamente, precisamente, esattamente
exaggerate esagerare
examine, to esaminare
example esempio
excellent eccellente, ottimo
except eccetto
excuse me! scusi!
excuse, to scusare
exist, to esistere
exit uscita
expensive caro

explain, to spiegare
export, to esportare
expression espressione *f.*
extinguish, to spegnere

F

fabric tessuto
face faccia
factory fabbrica
faithful fedele
fall caduta
family famiglia
famous famoso
far lontano, distante
    as ... as fino a
farm podere *m.*
farmer contadino, agricoltore *m.*
fashion moda
fast veloce
fat grasso
father padre *m.*
favorable favorevole
fear paura
February febbraio
feel sentire
festival festa
fever febbre *f.*
field campo
fifth quinto
fifteen quindici
fifty cinquanta
fill, to riempire
film film *m.*, pellicola
finally finalmente
find, to trovare
finger dito *(pl.* le dita*)*
finish, to finire
first primo
first class prima classe
fish pesce *m.*
fish, to pescare
five cinque
flame fiamma
floor (of a house) piano
flower fiore *m.*
fly, to volare
fog nebbia
follow, to seguire
food cibo

foot piede *m.*
footwear calzature *f. pl.*
for per
foreign estero
foreigner straniero, forestiero
forget, to dimenticare
forgive, to perdonare
fork forchetta
fortunate fortunato
forty quaranta
forward avanti
fountain fontana
four quattro
fourteen quottordici
fourth quarto
France Francia
free gratis, libero
freeze, to congelare
French francese *m. & f.*
frequently frequentemente
fresh fresco
Friday venerdì *m.*
fried fritto
friend amico
friendship amicizia
frightened, to be spaventarsi
from da
front, in davanti
frost gelo
fruit la frutta (at the table), frutto
fry, to friggere
funny comico, buffo
furnish, to arredare
furnished ammobiliato, arredato
furniture mobilia
    piece of ... mobile *m.*

G

game partita
garage rimessa, autorimessa, garage
garden giardino
gas gas *m.*
gather, to radunarsi, riunirsi
gentleman signore *m.*
German tedesco, tedeschi *pl.*
get up, to alzarsi
girdle panciera
girl ragazza, fanciulla
give, to dare, porgere
glad lieto, contento

glass bicchiere *m.*, vetro
glove guanto
go, to andare
go up, to salire
God Dio
gold oro
good buono
goodbye addio
granddaughter nipote *f.*
grandfather nonno
grandmother nonna
grandson nipote *m.*
grapefruit pompelmo
grape uva
grateful grato, riconoscente
grave grave
gray grigio
Greece Grecia
green verde
greet, to salutare
greeting saluto
group gruppo
grow, to crescere
guess, to indovinare
guest invitato
guide guida

H

hair capello, *pl.* capelli; pelo
half metà, mezzo
hall sala
ham (Italian) prosciutto
hammer martello
hand mano *f.*, lancetta (of a watch or clock)
handbag borsetta
handkerchief fazzoletto
happiness felicità
happy felice
hard duro
hat cappello
hate, to odiare
have, to avere
have to, to dovere
he egli
head testa, capo
health salute *f.*
hear, to udire
heart cuore *m.*
heat riscaldamento, calore *m.*

heavy pesante
heel tacco (*pl.* tacchi)
help aiuto
her, hers il suo, la sua, i suoi, le sue
here qui, qua
here is ecco, c'è
high alto
hill colle *m.*, collina
his, il suo, la sua, i suoi, le sue
history storia
hold, to tenere
holiday festa
Holland Olanda
holy santo
homeland patria
honest onesto
honey miele *m.*
honeymoon luna di miele
honeymoon trip viaggio di nozze
honor onore *m.*
hope speranza
hope, to sperare
horn (of a car) tromba
horse cavallo
hospital ospedale *m.*
hospitality ospitalità
hot caldo
hotel albergo
hour ora
house casa, stabile *m.*
how come, quanto
how much? quanto?
however però, ma, tuttavia
humidity umidità
hundred cento
hunger fame *f.*
hungry, to be avere appetito, avere fame
hurry fretta
husband marito

I

I io
ice ghiaccio
ice cream gelato
idea idea
if se
ignorance ignoranza
ignorant ignorante
ill malato, ammalato
I am . . . sto male

imagine, to immaginare
immediately immediatamente
import, to importare
important importante
impression impressione *f.*
impossible impossibile
impossibility impossibilità
in in
inasmuch as siccome, poichè, dato che
include, to includere
incorrect, scorretto, sbagliato
indeed in verità
indicate, to indicare
industrial industriale
industry industria
inexpensive a buon mercato
inform, to informare
inhabitant abitante *m.*
ink inchiostro
inside dentro
instead invece
insure, to assicurare
intelligent intelligente
interesting interessante
interrupt, to interrompere
intimate intimo
introduce, to presentare
introduction introduzione *f.*
invite, to invitare
island isola
Italian italiano
Italy Italia
itinerary itinerario

J

jacket giacca
jam marmellata
January gennaio
jealous geloso
Jewish ebreo
joke, to scherzare
joy gioia
July luglio
jump, to saltare
June giugno

K

keep, to tenere, conservare, mantenere

key chiave *f.*
kilogram chilo, chilogrammo
kilometer chilometro
kind buono, gentile *adj.*
kind specie *f.*
kindness bontà, gentilezza
king re *m.*
kiss bacio
kitchen cucina
knife coltello
knock, to battere, bussare
know, to conoscere, sapere
knowledge sapienza, conoscenza

L

lady signora
lake lago
lamb agnello
lamp lampada
lamp bulb lampadina
language lingua
large largo, grande, vasto
last ultimo
last, to durare
last week la settimana scorsa
late tardi
later più tardi
laugh, to ridere
laughter riso, ilarità
laundry lavanderia
lavatory gabinetto
law legge *f.*
Leaning Tower Torre Pendente *f.*
learn, to imparare
least, at almeno
leather pelle *f.*, cuoio
leave, to lasciare (permit), partire (depart)
left sinistra
leg gamba
legal legale
lemon limone *m.*
lend, to prestare
less meno
lesson lezione *f.*
let, to lasciare, permettere
letter lettera
lettuce lattuga
library biblioteca

lie bugia
lie, to mentire, dire bugie
life vita
lift, to alzare
light, to accendere
lightning lampo
like, to piacere
line fila, linea
linen lino
linens biancheria
lion leone *m.*
list lista
literature letteratura
little poco, piccolo
live, to abitare, vivere
living room salotto
load, to caricare
located, to be trovarsi
lodging alloggio
logical logico
London Londra
loud forte, ad alta voce
longing nostalgia
look for, to cercare
lose, to perdere
loud forte, alto
love amore
love, to amare
lover amante
low basso
luck fortuna
lunch colazione *f.*
lunch, to have fare colazione
luxury lusso

M

machine macchina
madam signora
magnificent magnifico
mahogany mogano
maid domestica
mail posta
mailbox buca delle lettere
major maggiore
majordomo maggiordomo
make, to fare
man uomo *(pl.,* uomini)
manage, to dirigere, amministrare
manager dirigente *m.*
    amministatore *m.*

manner modo, maniera
many tanti,-e
map pianta, carta geografica
marble marmo
March marzo
market mercato
marry, to sposare
marvel meraviglia
marvelous meraviglioso
marvelously meravigliosamente
Mass Messa
mathematician matematico
material stoffa, materiale *m.*
mattress materasso
maximum massimo
May maggio
maybe forse
mayor sindaco
me me
meal pasto
meaning significato
means mezzo
meantime, in the nel frattempo
meanwhile intanto
measure misura
measurement misura
meat carne *f.*
medicine medicina
medieval medioevale
meet, to incontrare, riunirsi
melodious melodioso
menu lista della vivande
merchandise merce *f.*
merchant commerciante *m.*
message messaggio
meter metro
microscope microscopio
midday mezzogiorno
middle mezzo
Middle Ages medio evo
midnight mezzanotte *f.*
mild mite
milk latte *m.*
million milione *m.*
mine il mio, la mia, i miei, le mie
minute minuto *(n. & adj.)*
mirror specchio
Miss signorina
mistake sbaglio, errore *m.*
mistaken, to be sbagliarsi
mister signor
mix, to mischiare, mescolare

model modello
moderate moderato
moderation moderazione *f.*
modern moderno
modest modesto
Monday lunedì *m.*
money denaro, danaro
month mese *m.*
monthly mensilmente
monument monumento
moon luna
moor moro
more più
morning mattina
most la maggior parte
mother madre, mamma
motion picture, motion picture
  theatre cinema *m.*
motor motore *m.*
motorcycle motocicletta
mountain montagna, monte *m.*
movable mobile
move, to muovere
movement (of a watch) meccanismo
movie camera macchina
  cinematografica
Mrs. signora
much molto
mud fango
museum museo
music musica
musician musicista *m. & f.*
must dovere
mutton castrato
my il mio, la mia, i miei, le mie
myself me

N

name nome *m.*
napkin tovagliolo
narrow stretto
nation nazione *f.*
national nazionale
nationality nazionalità *f.*
natural naturale
naturally naturalmente
navy marina
near vicino
necessary necessario
  it is . . . è necessario, bisogna che
necessity bisogno, necessità

neck collo
necktie cravatta
need bisogno
needle ago
neighbor vicino
neither . . . nor nè . . . nè
nephew nipote *m.*
never mai, non . . . *(verb)* . . . mai
nevertheless tuttavia, eppure
new nuovo
newlyweds sposini, novelli sposi
newspaper giornale *m.*
next prossimo, venturo
  . . . week la settimana prossima
niece nipote
night notte *f.*
nine nove
nineteen diciannove
ninety novanta
no no
nobody nessuno
noon mezzogiorno
no one nessuno
north nord *n.*, settentrionale *adj.*
note nota
notebook quaderno
nothing niente, nulla
notice, to notare
November novembre *m.*
now adesso, ora
number numero
nut noce (tree *m.*, fruit *f.*)
nylon nylon

O

object oggetto
occasion occasione *f.*
occupy, to occupare
occur, to accadere, avvenire,
  capitare
October ottobre *m.*
of di
offer, to offrire
office sede *f.* ufficio
  main . . . sede centrale
  branch . . . succursale *f.*
often spesso
oil olio
old vecchio
olive oliva
on sopra, su

once una volta
one uno,-a
only solo, soltanto, solamente
open, to aprire
opinion opinione *f.*
opposite contrario, opposto
or oppure, o
orange arancia (*pl.* arance)
other altro
otherwise oppure, altrimenti
our, ours nostro, nostra, nostri,
  nostre
ourselves noi stessi
out of order guasto
over sopra
overcoat soprabito
overshoes soprascarpe, calosce,
  galosce
owe, to dovere
own proprio
ox bue *m.*

P

package pacco
pain dolore *m.*, pena
paint pittura
paint, to dipingere, pitturare
painting pittura, quadro
pair paio (*pl.*, le paia)
palace palazzo
paper carta
parent genitore *m.*
Paris Parigi *f.*
park parco
part parte *f.*
pass, to passare
passport passaporto
pastime passatempo
path cammino
pattern modello
pay, to pagare
payment pagamento
peace pace *f.*
peasant contadino
pen penna
  fountain . . . penna stilografica
pencil matita, lapis *m.*
penicillin penicillina
people popolo, gente *f.*
pepper pepe *m.*

per cent per cento
perfect perfetto
perfectly perfettamente
performance rappresentazione *f.*
perfume profumo
perhaps chissà, forse
period periodo
person persona
personal personale
perspire, to sudare
perspiration sudore *m.*
petticoat sottana
phonograph fonografo
photograph fotografia
physician medico
picture quadro, fotografia
piece pezzo
pillow cuscino
pineapple ananasso
pitcher caraffa
place luogo, posto
plane, by in aereo
plant pianta
plate piatto
play, to giocare
play, to (an instrument) suonare
pleasant piacevole
please per piacere
pocket tasca
point punto
point, to indicare
Poland Polonia
police polizia
policeman agente *m.*
poor povero
Pope Papa *m.*
popular popolare
pork maiale *m.*
port porto
possible possibile
post office ufficio postale, posta
potato patata
powder cipria, polvere
powerful potente
pray, to pregare
precise preciso
prefer, to preferire
prepare, to preparare
prescription ricetta
present attuale (now)
  at . . . al momento

present, to presentare
preserve, to conservare
pretty grazioso, carino
price prezzo
prince principe *m.*
probably probabilmente
proceed, to procedere
profit guadagno
promise promessa
pronunciation pronuncia, pronunzia
protest protesta
protest, to protestare
public pubblico
punctual puntuale
purchase acquisto, compra
purchase, to acquistare, comprare
put, to mettere
put on, to mettersi, indossare

Q

quality qualità
quarter (of a city) contrada, quartiere *m.*
queen regina
question domanda
quick presto, subito
quickly presto, subito

R

race corsa
radio radio *f.*
railroad ferrovia
rain pioggia
rain, to piovere
raincoat impermeabile *m.*
raise, to alzare
rapid rapido
rare raro
rare (meat) al sangue
rate rata
rather alquanto, piuttosto
raw crudo
rayon rayon
razor rasoio
razor blade lametta
ready pronto
real proprio, vero

really proprio, propriamente, veramente, davvero
reason ragione *f.*
reasonable moderato, ragionevole
receipt ricevuta
receive, to ricevere, accogliere
recent recente
recently recentemente
red rosso
refrigerator frigorifero
refuse, to rifiutare
region regione *f.*
regret, to pentirsi
relative parente *m. & f.*
religion religione *f.*
religious religioso
remain, to rimanere, trattenersi, restare
remainder resto
remember, to ricordare, rammentare
remind, to ricordare, rammentare
Renaissance Rinascimento
rent pigione *f.*
rent, to prendere in affitto, prendere in noleggio
repair, to riparare
repeat, to ripetere
replace, to sostituire
representative rappresentante *m.*
republic repubblica
reserve, to prenotare
reservation prenotazione *f.*
rest, to riposarsi
restaurant ristorante *m.*
retail al minuto
return, to ritornare
ribbon nastro
rice riso
rich ricco
right, to the a destra
ring, to (the hour) suonare
rise, to sorgere, alzarsi
river fiume *m.*
road strada
roast arrosto
roast beef arrosto di bue
rob, to rubare
roll rullino (film); rullo panino (bread)
room camera, stanza, vano (empty), sala

rose rosa
round rotondo
round trip andata e ritorno
row fila
rubbers calosce, galosce, soprascarpe
rug tappeto
ruins rovine, ruderi
rule, to governare
Rumania Rumenia
run, to correre
Russia Russia
Russian russo

S

sacrifice sacrificio
sail imbarcarsi
saint santo
salad insalata
salt sale m.
salty salato
same stesso
satisfy, to soddisfare
Saturday sabato
sauce salsa
saucer piattino
save, to risparmiare
say, to dire
scene scena
school scuola
science scienza
scientist scienziato
scissors forbici f.pl.
scream grido
sea mare m.
seashore lido
season stagione f.
seasoning condimento
seat sedile m.
second secondo
section (of a city) quartiere m.
  contrada
see, to vedere
seek, to cercare
seem, to sembrare
sell, to vendere
send, to spedire, mandare, inviare
September settembre m.
serious grave
serve, to servire
set, to apparecchiare

seven sette
seventeen diciassette
seventh settimo
seventy settanta
several diversi, diverse f.
sew, to cucire
sewing machine macchina da
  cucire
shade ombra
shadow ombra
sharp piccante
shave, to radere, farsi la barba
she ella, essa
ship piroscafo, vapore m., nave f.
shirt camicia (pl. camicie)
shoe scarpa
shop bottega (pl. botteghe)
short breve, corto, basso
shorts mutande f. pl.
show, to mostrare, dimostrare,
  far vedere
shower doccia, acquazzone
  (rain) m.
shoulder spalla
shout, to gridare
sick ammalato
  I feel ... sto male
  to get ... ammalarsi
side lato, parte f.
sidewalk marciapiede m.
sign segno, cartello
silence silenzio
silver argento
silk seta
similar simile
simple semplice
simply semplicemente
since siccome, poichè, giacchè
sing, to cantare
single solo, unico
sister sorella
sister-in-law cognata
sit, to sedersi
six sei
sixteen sedici
sixth sesto
sixty sessanta
size misura, numero
skin pelle f.
skirt gonnella

sleep, to dormire
   to go to ... addormentarsi
sleeve manica (pl. maniche)
slip sottana
slip, to scivolare
slow lento
small piccolo
smell, to odorare
smile, to sorridere
smoke, to fumare
smooth liscio
sneeze, to starnutire, starnutare
snow neve f.
so così (therefore, thus)
   ... much tanto
soap sapone m.
sock calzino
sofa divano
soldier soldato, milite m.
some alcuni,-e
some un po', un po' di
somebody qualcuno
someone qualcuno
sometimes qualche volta
something qualche cosa
somewhat alquanto
son figlio
song canzone f.
soon presto
   as ... as appena
soup brodo, zuppa
south sud n., meridionale adj.
souvenir ricordo
spaghetti spaghetti
Spain Spagna
Spaniard Spagnuolo
Spanish spagnuolo
speak, to parlare
special speciale
spend, to (time) passare,
   (money) spendere
sponge spugna
spoon cucchiaio
spring molla, primavera
square piazza
stairs scale
stairway scala
stamp francobollo, bollo
stand up, to stare in piedi
state stato
start, to iniziare, incominciare
station stazione f.

stay permanenza
stay, to alloggiare, stare
steak bistecca
steal, to rubare
steamboat vapore m.
steward maggiordomo
still ancora
stocking calza
stomach stomaco
stone pietra, sasso
stop, to fermare
store negozio bottega
storm tempesta
story storia
story (of a house) piano, (tale) storia
straight diritto, dritto
strange strano
street via, strada
strike, to battere
strong forte
study studio
study, to studiare
stove stufa
student studente m., studentessa f.
stupid stupido
style stile m.
sublime sublime
sudden repentino, improvviso
sugar zucchero
suit abito, vestito
suitcase valigia (pl. valigie)
summer estate f., estivo adj.
sun sole m.
Sunday domenica
sunset tramonto
supper cena
supper, to have cenare
suppose, to supporre
sure sicuro
sweet dolce
swim, to nuotare
Swiss svizzero

T

table tavola
tablecloth tovaglia
tailor sarto
tailor shop sartoria
take, to prendere
   ... the measurement prendere
   la misura

take off, to (aviation) decollare
tall alto
taste gusto
taste, to assaggiare, gustare
tax tassa
taxi tassì *m.*
teach, to insegnare
teacher maestro
tear lagrima
tear, to lacerare, stracciare
teaspoon cucchiaino
telegraph to, telegrafare
telegram telegramma *m.*
telephone telefono
telephone, to telefonare
television televisione *f.*
tell, to dire, narrare
temperature temperatura
ten dieci
tenth decimo
than che, di
thank, to ringraziare
thank you grazie
that che *conj.,* quello *pro. & adj.*
the il, lo, la, i, gli, le
theater teatro
them loro, essi, esse, li, le
then poi, allora
there là, ci, vi
there are ci sono, ecco
there is c'è, ecco
therefore quindi, perciò, dunque
thermometer termometro
they loro, essi, esse
thin sottile, magro
think, to pensare
third terzo
thirteen tredici
thirst sete *f.*
thirty trenta
this questo
thought pensiero
thousand (*pl.* mila)
thousands migliaia
thread filo
threaten, to minacciare
three tre
throw, to lanciare, gettare, buttare
thunder tuono
Thursday giovedì
thus così

ticket biglietto
ticket window biglietteria
tight stretto
time ora, tempo
    on . . . a tempo, in tempo
timetable orario
tip mancia, punta
tired stanco
to a
tobacco tabacco
today oggi
together insieme, assieme
toilet gabinetto
tomato pomodoro
tomb tomba
tomorrow domani
tongue lingua
tonight stasera
too anche, pure
    too much troppo
tooth dente *m.*
toothbrush spazzolino
toothpaste dentrifricio
top cima
total totale
touch, to toccare
tough duro
tourist turista *m.*
towel asciugamano
trade commercio
traffic traffico
train treno
translate, to tradurre
transport, to trasportare
transportation trasporto
travel, to viaggiare
traveler viaggiatore
tree albero
trip viaggio, gita
trousers calzoni *m.pl.*
truck autocarro, camion
true vero
trunk baule *m.*
truth verità
try, to provare
try on, to provare
Tuesday martedì
Turkey Turchia
turn off the light, to spegnere la
    luce
turn over, to voltare
typewriter macchina da scrivere

typewrite, to scrivere a macchina
twelve dodici
twenty venti
two due

U

ugly brutto
umbrella ombrello, parapioggia *m.*
uncle zio
under sotto
understand, to capire
underwear biancheria intima,
   mutande
undoubtedly indubbiamente
undress, to svestirsi, spogliarsi
unfortunately purtroppo
united unito
United States Stati Uniti *m. pl.*
university università
unless a meno che
until fino a
up, to go salire, andar sù
upon sopra
urgent urgente
us ci
use uso
use, to usare
useful utile
useless inutile
usual solito
usually generalmente, di solito

V

vacation vacanza
vain, in invano
valid valido
value valore *m.*
variety varietà
Vatican Vaticano
vegetables legumi *m.pl.*, verdura
vehicle veicolo
very molto
vest panciotto
victory vittoria
view veduta, panorama *m.*
visit visita
visit, to visitare
voice voce *f.*
voyage viaggio

W

waist cintura, vita
waistline vita
wait, to aspettare
waiter cameriere *m.*
waiting room sala d'aspetto
wake up, to svegliarsi
walk passeggiata, passeggio
walk, to passeggiare, camminare
wall muro
want, to volere
war guerra
warm caldo
warn, to avvertire
wash, to lavare
wash oneself, to lavarsi
wash basin lavabo
waste, to sprecare
watch orologio
watchmaker orologiaio
water acqua
wave onda
way, this da questa parte
we noi
wealth ricchezza
weather tempo
Wednesday mercoledì
week settimana
weigh, to pesare
weigh oneself, to pesarsi
weight peso
welcome! benvenuto!
welcome, to accogliere
well bene
west ovest *m.*, ponente *m.*
what che, ciò che (that which)
what? che cosa?
whatever qualunque cosa
wheat grano
wheel ruota
when quando
whenever qualora
where dove
   ... is? dov'è?
which che, quale
which? quale?
while mentre
white bianco
who che
who? chi
whoever chiunque

wholesale all'ingrosso
whom che, chi
why? perchè?
wide largo
wife sposa, moglie, signora
wind vento
wind, to caricare
window finestra
wine vino
winter inverno
wish desiderio, augurio
wish, to augurare, desiderare, volere
with con
within dentro
without senza
wolf lupo
woman donna
wonder meraviglia
wonderful meraviglioso, magnifico
wood legno
woods bosco
wool lana
word parola
work lavoro, opera
   ... of art opera d'arte
world mondo
   of the ... mondiale

worry preoccupazione *f.*
worse peggiore, *adj.* peggio *adv.*
wrap, to avvolgere
wrist polso
write, to scrivere
writer scrittore *m.*, scrittrice *f.*

Y Z

year anno
yellow giallo
yes sì
yesterday ieri
yet ancora
you tu, lei, voi, loro
young giovane
young lady signorina
your il suo, la sua, i suoi, le sue
   (pol. sing.)
   il loro, la loro, i loro, le loro
   (pol. pl.)
   il tuo, la tua, i tuoi, le tue
   (fam. sing.)
   il vostro, la vostra, i vostri,
   le vostre *(fam. pl.)*
zero zero